Choose Your Life
A Travel Guide for Living

Illustrations by Sabrina Melo da Silva

Choose Your Life

A Travel Guide for Living

KAREN GEDIG BURNETT

GR Publishing
Felton, California
www.GRPBooks.com

Choose Your Life
By Karen Gedig Burnett

Copyright © GR Publishing, 2008 Choose Your Life.

GR Publishing, Felton, California
www.GRPBooks.com

Publisher's Note: Names have been changed to protect the innocent (and the guilty).

Cover and interior design © TLC Graphics, www.TLCGraphics.com
Design by Monica Thomas

Publisher's Cataloging-in-Publication
(Provided by Quality Books, Inc.)

Burnett, Karen Gedig.
    Choose your life: a travel guide for living / by
Karen Gedig Burnett; illustrations by Sabrina Melo da Silva.
    p. cm.
    Includes index.
    LCCN 2006911219
    ISBN-13: 9780966853070
    ISBN-10: 0966853075

    1. Self-perception. 2. Self-actualization (Psychology)
I. Silva, Sabrina Melo da, ill. II. Title.

BF697.5.S43B87 2007   158.1
                                   QBI07-600062

Printed in the United States of America.

Acknowledgments

How do I even begin to thank all the people who have contributed to the development of this book? In many ways this book has been in the making for over 50 years. A simple statement, a conversation, or a question may have led to small additions or major changes.

First I want to thank my family. My husband, Henry J. Burnett, has been my main sounding board. He once said, "I don't think I will need to read the book. I've heard it all before." I want to thank Trevor, Clare, and Gavin. I have benefited by being connected to each of them. I want to thank them for their support and help. Trevor was the first person I turned to with a spelling question.

Next I want to acknowledge the people most involved in the development and creation of this book. I want to thank my editor, Joanne Sperans Hartzell. She stayed with me through my multiple revisions, always providing patience and support. Her enthusiasm for this project showed, and I thank her for helping make my message clear and concise.* Sabrina Melo da Silva, my illustrator, was a godsend. I absolutely love the way she complemented my messages with her creative and entertaining illustrations. And last in this group, but not least, I want to thank my graphic artist, Monica Thomas of TLC Graphics, for creating a wonderful design and flow to this book. She really tied everything together.

Several people played a major role in the development and completion of this book. They volunteered time and energy in helping with the many revisions, and their contributions were invaluable. Thank you Beverly Merkley, Susie Beaty, Becky Dalton, Carol Gedig, Kurt Gedig, Frank Adamson, Ellen Kimmel, Jana Merrill, Marilyn Schuler, Veronica Riglick, June Gorman, and Laurey Campbell.

Other people contributed through discussions, encouragement, or suggestions. Thank you Teresa Martinez, Bette Simpson, Jane Madsen, Debbie Bourne, Shirley Zink, Judy Thompson, Judy Hunt, Ron Campbell, Candice Arndt, Marian Vargas, Anne Dotson, Gini Gyorkos, Anne Walker, Doug Walker, Dunkin, and Zoë.

I would also like to thank the students and staff at Rescue School for providing meaningful challenges and inspiration.

And finally, I want to thank my father, John E. Gedig. In a recent conversation, as we talked about the passing of my mother in 2003, I saw him transition through his emotions. He started with a tear, fairly quickly moved on to acceptance, and then focused on the present. As I watched I realized that the ideas presented in this book are basically an extension of his approach to life. I have been learning from him my whole life. Thank you Dad. I am lucky to be your daughter.

This book is written in conversational style. Literary license was taken by the author and may not have been the recommendation of the editor.

Introduction

Welcome to a book that can change your life. *Choose Your Life: A Travel Guide for Living* contains tips on how to view life, ways to handle difficulties, and tools to help increase your happiness. Ideas are presented in a simple and graphic manner easily understood by those who are young, yet the ideas are valuable to people of all ages.

So who am I and how did this book originate?

My name is Karen Gedig Burnett. I was an elementary school counselor for over 20 years. Fairly early in my career I started telling stories to help students learn about themselves and how to handle difficulties. I realized I had a talent for taking complex ideas and making them 'seeable,' and therefore easier to understand. Some of my stories became children's books, and as of this date I have four published books dealing with life skills.

As my books were published I began speaking at other schools, sharing the messages contained in the stories. Although my primary audience was often elementary students, adults would invariably come forward with comments such as: "This helped me more than it helped my students (or child)." Or, "I needed to hear that. It will help me deal with...."

Or, "I wish I had learned this when I was younger." Or, "You should do something like this for adults." One person even said, "I've been in therapy for six years, but you helped me more in one hour than [therapy did] in all that time." So although I was often speaking to children, adults benefited from my messages as well. That's when I realized that I needed to write this book.

Choose Your Life: A Travel Guide for Living is a compilation of ideas and approaches to life that I have learned, created, or revised to help make life easier. Some ideas were gleaned from others, some were developed when I first started creating programs at schools almost 30 years ago, and some of them were developed as this book evolved.

Choose Your Life will help in all phases and facets of life.

It's for teens as they begin choosing their directions in life, but it's also for adults as they continue making life-changing choices.

Although the book can help people facing major decisions, it's primarily for everyone as we make daily choices that influence our life, as these small, daily decisions may lead to major decisions.

It can help parents as they guide their young children, or even as they deal with their grown-up children.

It can be used by families to read and discuss together.

Choose Your Life will help you better understand relationships with family, friends, co-workers, and even casual acquaintances. But mainly it will help you with the most important relationship of all—your relationship with yourself.

So read to help yourself. Read to help others. Read to guide the next generation.

Start at the beginning and read to the end, or just flip through until something catches your eye.

Write in the margins and date it. (Later you will be glad you did.) You will change through the years. Whether you go from 16 to 19 or 51 to 54, you will change. That's what life is about: changing, learning, and growing.

This multi-generational book provides guidance for a lifetime.

You will embrace some ideas right away and see them as useful. Other ideas you will just skim over. Every time you read this book you will take something different from the suggestions. And you will find that the ideas you passed over at one time will provide much-needed guidance at another point in your life.

Throughout, you will learn to develop thoughts and attitudes that will help you choose the life you want and love the life you choose.

I hope you have a wonderful journey.

Karen Gedig Burnett

Contents

Choose Your Life:

The Anatomy of Making Choices

The greatest power that a person possesses
is the power to choose.

J. Martin Kohe, Author and Psychologist (1902–)

You may have a fresh start any moment you choose,
for this thing that we call 'failure' is not the falling down,
but the staying down.

Mary Pickford, Actress (1893–1979)

Understand that the right to choose your own path
is a sacred privilege. Use it.

*Oprah Winfrey, Entertainment Executive, Talk Show Host,
Magazine Publisher. and Actress (1954–)*

It's choice–not chance–that determines your destiny.

Jean Nidetch, Co-founder of Weight Watchers International (1927–)

Life is what we make it, always has been, always will be.

*Grandma Moses (Anna Mary Robertson),
American Folk Artist (1860–1961)*

People often say that this or that person has not found himself.
But the self is not something one finds.
It is something that one creates.

*Thomas Szasz
Psychiatry Professor and Author (1920–)*

1

Some Basics

*Y*ou make millions of choices each day: from little choices (do you eat a hot dog or a hamburger), to bigger choices (do you clean the house today or tomorrow), to even bigger choices (do you stay in school, do you have sex, do you quit your job).

Sometimes your life can totally change as the result of one big choice. But most of the time, the direction your life takes is based upon many little choices—little choices that add up.

The first time Tina went to her real estate class, she felt overwhelmed. But then she studied a little every day and sometimes asked for help. By the time the test came, she knew she would do okay.

◆ ◆ ◆

Marco used his new credit card to buy little things. It was no big deal. There was $5 here and $20 there. The biggest thing he bought was just $50. "Heck," he thought, "I'm not buying that much." Plus, he felt *powerful when he used his credit card, like he could buy anything. Then Marco got his bill. He was shocked to see he owed $678. He didn't have that much money to spare. Now what was he going to do?*

Each choice by itself may seem trivial, but as they add up they can have a major impact. Just like each piece of clothing you drop on your bedroom floor may not seem like much, but 'suddenly' (after several days) you have a huge mess.

And even if you look at the biggest choice you have made in life, this big choice was preceded by many little choices that got you to that point.

How your choices ADD UP determines your life.

Your choices can add up to bring you happiness or cause you pain. They affect how you view the world and how the world views you. Your choices can add up to success or to ongoing struggles.

So although you might prepare for and think a lot about the big choices you face, mostly it's the little choices you make every day that add up to determine your life.

When we want our life to go in a different direction, we often want it to happen **NOW**. But usually, changing your life's direction doesn't happen quickly; it takes time and effort. It involves many little steps in the new direction. But if you don't take those steps in a different direction, where will you be days, weeks, or even months from now?

Think about where you want your life to head. What little step can you make today to improve your chances of getting there?

That's all it takes to get started. One little step at a time. Things will start to change in a positive direction. The same is true, however, for your life to change in a negative direction. It takes some little action in an unproductive direction, or even inaction, to reduce your chances for success as well. But even then, you can always choose a different step.

So, if you want your life to be different, start by changing just one thing, keep doing it, be patient, and watch it ADD UP from there.

SOME BASIC FACTS ABOUT MAKING CHOICES

◆ Some people tend to choose quickly and others take a long time to think things over. Most of us do a little of both.

◆ You could take a long time to decide something that won't matter hours later. But then again you could make a quick decision about something that totally changes your life.

◆ Sometimes you wish you could change your mind or go back in time and do things differently. You can spend endless hours rehashing your past and beating yourself up for a choice you made. But the past is over; what is done is done, and no matter how much you think about it, you can't change it. But you CAN learn from it and make a choice NOW that can change your future.

◆ Sometimes you choose not to choose—which really is a choice in itself. And when you choose not to choose, others may step in to make a decision for you.

◆ Sometimes you choose to do nothing—which is also a choice. Later you may be glad or you may regret that you didn't act.

(continues on next page)

(continued from previous page)

◆ For many choices there are short-term effects and long-term effects. What may look easiest or best for the short term (the next couple of minutes) may not be what is best in the long term (later today, next week, or even next year).

◆ Every situation is different. What might be an easy choice at one time may be a hard choice at another. And everybody is different. What may be an easy choice for you could be difficult for someone else. And vice versa.

◆ Some choices will be clear and easy. But other choices will be complex with many factors to think about.

We all face difficult decisions at some time in life.

◆ When talking about a friend, you said something you now regret. Now what do you do?

◆ You know that your best friend's 'special someone' is not being honest and faithful. Do you say something?

◆ Someone asks you a personal question in front of a group. How do you respond?

◆ You are with a friend and they do something illegal or unethical. So what do you do?

◆ The boss at your new job tells dirty jokes and everyone laughs. You don't feel comfortable. Do you confront your boss?

◆ Your friends make fun of someone who is mentally challenged. Do you join in or tell them to stop?

◆ Someone pressures you to act in a way that doesn't feel right. What do you do next?

◆ A friend does something wrong and asks you to cover for them. Do you?

◆ Family members argue and want you to take sides. What do you do?

When faced with difficult choices it can be hard to think clearly. You wish you could just call **time out** and step back and think things through.

DECISIONS CAN BE DIFFICULT WHEN:

They are NEW EXPERIENCES.

You are caught off guard. You have never thought about or planned what you would do in a situation like this. So now you are trying to consider all the factors involved to help you make your decision.

You feel BOMBARDED.

Right now life feels out of control. There are too many things happening at one time, and your thoughts are spinning.

You feel TIME PRESSURE.

You feel pressured to make a decision NOW. This pressure can be coming from you, or it could be coming from others.

You have an INTERNAL CONFLICT.

Part of you wants to do one thing, and the other part wants to do something else; or you feel unsure and confused.

(continues on next page)

(continued from previous page)

You're IN THE SPOTLIGHT.

Everybody seems to be watching to see what you do.

You feel THE WEIGHT OF THE WORLD.

You feel pressured within yourself to make the 'right' choice, (as if there is a 'right' choice). Or you think your decision has a major effect on other people's lives and happiness. So this decision feels heavy.

You feel PRESSURE FROM OTHERS.

Others are pressuring you to either make a choice or even do what they want. You are not sure what you want, or you don't want to let them down, or you want to please them, so you feel confused and stressed.

The decision requires you to STAND UP.

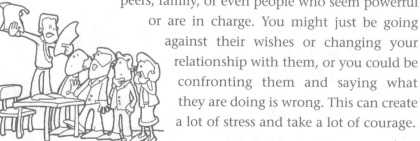

To do what you think is right, you would have to stand up to friends, peers, family, or even people who seem powerful or are in charge. You might just be going against their wishes or changing your relationship with them, or you could be confronting them and saying what they are doing is wrong. This can create a lot of stress and take a lot of courage.

The more confusion, the more voices (yours and others') telling you what to do, the more emotion—the greater the stress. And when you're stressed, it's hard to think clearly. In fact, at times like these, even simple decisions may seem difficult.

Why is it hard to think clearly when you feel STRESSED?

Why does it seem like your brain shuts down? Why do you act, only to wonder later, "Why did I do that?" or "What was I thinking?" The truth is you probably weren't thinking—at least not clearly. You weren't using all your mental abilities.

Let me explain.

The Three Parts of Your Brain

The first part, your Primitive Survival Brain, handles basic survival: alertness, body temperature, hunger, heartbeat, and reflexes. It is where your instinctual fears are stored and is the center that controls your fight-or-flight fear reflex. These responses are automatic, with no thought. Lizards and snakes, for example, have a Primitive Survival Brain.

The second part, your Intermediate Emotional Brain, handles emotions. It covers everything from attraction and attachment to others, to social ties, to fears. Since we learn and remember best when there is

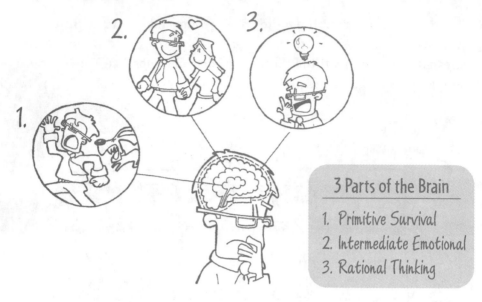

3 Parts of the Brain

1. Primitive Survival
2. Intermediate Emotional
3. Rational Thinking

an emotional element involved, emotional memories play a strong role in our life. This includes memories not only of security and comfort, but especially those involving fear. Dogs, cats, monkeys, and other mammals have both a Survival Brain and an Emotional Brain.

The third part, your Rational Thinking Brain, handles complex social interactions. It gives you the ability to reason, understand past experiences, plan for the future, and analyze and solve problems. You use this part of your brain to learn and think. Although some other animals have this third brain, none is as well-developed as the human Thinking Brain.

It is not the strongest of the species that survives, nor the most intelligent, but the one most responsive to change.

Charles Darwin,
British Scientist (1809–1882)

So when you want to handle a problem the best you can, which brain would you want to use? **Your Thinking Brain.**

But scientists have found the more stressed you feel, the more your Thinking Brain shuts down. So when you are really stressed, you are left making decisions with your Survival Brain and Emotional Brain. The responses from these two brains are almost totally automatic and devoid of higher thinking, so they don't usually make the best decisions. It's not their strength.

In essence, when you are stressed you lose your most valuable asset, your Thinking Brain. This would be like losing your best player when there are 10 seconds left and the game is tied.

So what happens when you are stressed and you can't think straight?

◆ You just react, often handling the problem the same way you have always handled it or the way you have seen it handled before by others.

◆ You give in and just do what others want, ignoring your intuition or own concerns or wishes.

◆ You avoid the problem and get involved in something else: work, play, friends, television, eating, shopping, partying, drugs, or alcohol.

◆ You deny you have a problem and totally ignore it. So, in your mind, 'poof,' it just disappears.

◆ You freeze and do nothing or sit and worry—which feels like you are doing something.

◆ You procrastinate, say you will deal with the problem later, and then keep putting it off.

All of these solutions may temporarily eliminate your feelings of stress. But, since none of them involve using your Thinking Brain, they usually don't solve the problem. They are short-term solutions. But what happens in the long run?

◆ When you just react or handle the problem the same way you've always handled it, that doesn't usually solve the problem. It may disappear for a while, but it returns and is usually bigger.

◆ When you avoid a problem or procrastinate, your problem doesn't go away, it just keeps adding up.

◆ When you give in and just do what people want, ignoring your intuition, concerns, or wishes, you may resolve one problem—pressure from others. But now you have a different, even bigger problem—you weren't true to yourself.

So when you don't use your Thinking Brain to solve your problems, they don't magically disappear. They may just change for a while, and often get bigger. This creates more stress and makes it harder to use your Thinking Brain to solve your problem.

> We must not, in trying to think about how we can make a big difference, ignore the small daily differences we can make which, over time, add up to big differences that we often cannot foresee.
>
> *Marian Wright Edelman*
> *American Activist and Founder of*
> *Children's Defense Fund (1939–)*

It's a vicious cycle. Stress—can't think—temporary solution—problem changes or gets bigger—creates more stress—can't think—and on and on we go.

When you use your Thinking Brain, you open up your options. You analyze and think things through, which can help you find new and better ways to solve problems. You learn from the past and plan new approaches for the future. When you do this, you improve your chances of finding both short-term and long-term solutions that would truly work.

Using your Thinking Brain is vital to helping you choose the life you want to lead.

So this Rational Thinking Brain of yours is a wonderful thing.

But wait, the same Thinking Brain that helps you solve problems can also create problems.

What is the only animal that worries about paperwork, or a grade, or getting to work on time, or bills, or getting a raise?

What is the only animal that worries if someone's talking about them, or doesn't like them, or whether they are loved or wanted?

> It's not what's happening to you now or what has happened in your past that determines who you become. Rather, it's your decisions about what to focus on, what things mean to you, and what you're going to do about them that will determine your ultimate destiny.
>
> *Anthony Robbins*
> *(Anthony J. Mahavorick),*
> *Life Coach, Writer, and*
> *Motivational Speaker (1960–)*

What is the only animal that worries about their health, their wealth, their bathroom habits, or even their death?

HUMANS!

This wonderful Thinking Brain that we have to help us solve problems is also used to create problems.

Humans think about this and worry about that. They dissect and reanalyze bits and pieces of their lives, creating stress with their own thoughts.

So, what can we do?

We need our Thinking Brain to help us analyze and develop new and useful solutions to our problems, thus reducing stress.

But at the same time, our Thinking Brain can create worries and problems that increase our stress.

This book will continue to show you how to use your Thinking Brain effectively, reduce your stress, recognize what is best for you, and make choices that truly improve your life.

But first, here is an important fact to remember.

You will make mistakes. So don't be too hard on yourself.

No matter whether you act quickly or think things through, take action or do nothing, or use your full abilities or not, you will make mistakes. It's just a fact of life. You make mistakes because YOU ARE NOT PERFECT (surprise, surprise). Nobody is.

> Your life only gets better, when **you** get better!
>
> *Brian Tracy, Business and Personal Management Author and Speaker (1944–)*

Everyone makes mistakes. Sometimes people make the same mistake over and over until they finally learn how to handle their lives differently.

Now you could get mad at yourself when you make a mistake, but that usually doesn't help.

Getting mad at yourself helps only if you use that energy to go forward and make improvements. But if all you do is get mad, criticize, berate, or condemn yourself (or others), that is a total waste of your time and energy.

THINK ABOUT IT

If you mess up a project, lose a job, or blow a test, does getting mad make it better, or does it just make you miserable? When you are miserable, do you usually act or do your best? What could you learn from this to help you in the future?

If you say something that you wish you hadn't said or forget to do something you promised, does getting mad at yourself make it better? Does getting mad improve your relationship with others or just make you less desirable to be with? What could you do differently in the future?

Getting mad at yourself for something you did in the past (even one second ago is the past) doesn't change the past. It only affects how you feel and act in the present. And if you stay upset, it will affect the future.

The best you can do is go forward. Every mistake you make is just an opportunity to learn, to use your Thinking Brain to figure out how to make your life better.

Take steps to correct your mistake, if you can, and then look forward and figure out how you can move your life in a positive direction.

You see, you are not Perfect,
but you are Perfectly Human.

In the middle of difficulty lies opportunity.

Albert Einstein, U.S. (German-born) Physicist (1879–1955)

Every man is the architect of his own fortune.

Appius Claudius, Roman Politician (340–273 B.C.)

Whatever you fear most has no power—
it is your fear that has the power.

*Oprah Winfrey, Entertainment Executive, Talk Show Host,
Magazine Publisher. and Actress (1954–)*

When you make a mistake, don't look back at it long.
Take the reason of the thing into your mind
and then look forward.
Mistakes are lessons of wisdom.
The past cannot be changed.
The future is yet in your power.

Hugh White, U.S. Politician (1773–1840)

You don't get to choose how you're going to die. Or when.
You can only decide how you're going to live.

Joan Baez, Folk Singer (1941–)

Sometimes even to live is an act of courage.

*Seneca, Roman Dramatist, Philosopher,
and Politician (5 B.C.–65 A.D.)*

2

Pressure from People

Throughout life there will be give and take. Sometimes things will go the way you want, and sometimes things will go the way other people want.

- You want to do the project one way and others in your group have a different idea.
- You want to go to a movie and your friend wants to go to a party.
- You want to sit quietly and read and someone else wants to talk.

There just isn't any pleasing some people. The trick is to stop trying.

Robert Mitchum,
American Actor and Singer
(1917–1997)

But sometimes people are so focused on what they want that they fail to consider another person's position. They try to persuade, pressure, or manipulate others into doing what they want.

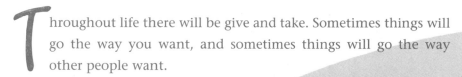

TRICKS PEOPLE USE TO TRY TO GET THEIR WAY:

They TALK (and talk, and talk...)

They keep talking and explaining, hoping that you keep listening, so they can convince you or wear you down until you do what they want.

They Bend the TRUTH.

They distort the truth or even make things up. Some people will say anything to get you to do what they want.

They BRIBE.

They offer to do things for you, or give you things, or trade with you, all to try to get you to do what they want.

They BEG.

They plead and beg. "Please. Just this once? I'll never ask again. Please."

They Become Your BEST FRIEND.

They become so nice and friendly. For this short time they act like they are your best friend...until they get what they want.

Don't mess it up for all of us.

We need one more person.

Come on. It will just take a couple of hours.

They INVOLVE OTHERS.

They either talk about how other people are on their side or try to get other people who are on their side to actually pressure you. They hope that group pressure will work to get you to do what they want.

They PLAY on Your EMOTIONS.

Although most of the tricks mentioned so far play on your emotions, people may primarily focus on your emotions to try to get you to do what they want. They may try to make you feel:

BAD If you feel bad enough, maybe you will give in and do what they want.

GUILTY They act like you are responsible for their pain, especially if you don't do what they want.

SORRY FOR THEM They want you to feel sorry for them, even pity them, so you will do what they want to 'make' them feel better.

SCARED They threaten to do something you don't want, like exclude you, take something away, leave, or even hurt you.

And Finally — They May Try FORCE!!

Some people even try to overpower you, to force you to do what they want.

WARNING It is NOT okay for someone to hurt you or force you to do things against your will. Stand up for yourself, and if you need to, report these people to someone who can help. If you are an adult or out of school you would want to contact the police. If you are still in school you might want to talk with a parent, a teacher, a counselor, or a police officer.

Manipulative Tricks:

- Keep talking
- Bend the truth
- Bribe
- Beg
- Act really nice
- Involve others
- Try to make you feel bad, guilty, sorry or scared
- Use force

The sole purpose of these manipulative tricks is to, well, manipulate you. The other person puts pressure on you and tries to wear you down, catch you off guard, confuse you, or get your emotions stirred up because then they hope to have some control and get you to do what they want.

? ? QUESTIONS FOR YOU

◆ Think of someone who is easily manipulated. How do people try to manipulate them, what tricks do they use? Why do you think it is easy to manipulate this person?

◆ Now think of someone who is not easily manipulated. What happens when people try some of these manipulative tricks? Why do you think it isn't easy for others to manipulate this person?

◆ Now think about yourself. Who can easily manipulate you? What tricks do they use? Why do you find it hard to stand up to them?

◆ Who cannot easily manipulate you? What tricks do they try to use? Why is it easy to stand up to them?

◆ Who can you easily manipulate? What tricks do you try?

◆ Who is not easily manipulated by you? What happens when you try to manipulate them?

◆ How are these two people different?

If someone uses any of these tricks to get you to do what they want, and it works, what do you think they will do the next time they want something from you?

You've heard the saying, "Fool me once, shame on you. Fool me twice, shame on me." Recognize when someone is trying to manipulate you, and learn what you can do to be true to yourself the next time.

Respect yourself!

? ?

The ME-MEs

When people try these manipulative tricks on you, who are they thinking about?

◆ Are they thinking about you—how you feel, what you want, what's best for you?

— or —

◆ Are they thinking about themselves—what they want and how they can get what they want?

Ding Ding Ding Ding and the answer is:

They are thinking about THEMSELVES. They are thinking about the big **ME**.

They are ME-MEs.

We are all ME-MEs to some extent. We think mostly of ourselves, because, well, that's where our brain is. We think about what is happening in our lives, our wishes, our problems, what we want, and how to get what we want.

The question isn't how much you think about yourself; the question is, how much do you consider others, too?

Do you consider other people's feelings and wishes?

Do you push others around to get what you want?

> We probably wouldn't worry about what people think of us if we could know how seldom they do.
>
> *Olin Miller*

Remember, no matter what tricks people use, no matter how much others pressure you to do what they want, *it's still your choice.*

If they are trying to manipulate you to get what they want, who are they thinking about?

And if you are worried about them and how they view you and whether they will be upset or not, who are YOU thinking about?

OUTSIDE PRESSURE and INSIDE PRESSURE

hen dealing with other people there are two types of pressure: pressure that comes from others (Outside Pressure) and pressure that comes from within you (Inside Pressure).

Outside Pressure comes from others as they try to persuade or force you to do what they want.

Inside Pressure comes from your own thoughts and worries about what you should do, what others may think, how you fit in, or how others view you.

Who Is Thinking About Whom?

When people use outside pressure, often they aren't thinking about you, how you feel, or what you want; they are mainly thinking about themselves, what they want, and how they can get you to do what they want.

Tim isn't thinking about what Jamie wants. He is thinking about how he could get Jamie to do what he wants. He is thinking about himself.

When your thoughts create inside pressure, you are also focused on the other person. You may be thinking about what they want and be worried about how they view you or whether you fit in or not. Often you are more concerned with what the other person thinks than with what you want for yourself.

> Sometimes a kid says they will be your friend if you give them your fruit snack. So you give it to them. They are real nice while they are eating it. Then they go away. But I think friends should last longer than a fruit snack.
>
> *Cary (age 8)*

Jamie is also thinking about Tim. She worries that he might get upset or stop liking her if she doesn't do what he wants.

So Tim is thinking about himself and Jamie is thinking about Tim.

So who is thinking about Jamie?

Now to be perfectly honest, Jamie IS thinking about Jamie! But she's NOT thinking, *"What do I want?"* Or, *"What feels right for me?"* She IS thinking, *"What if Tim doesn't like ME?"* And *"What if he gets mad at ME?"* Jamie is more concerned with Tim's perception of her and his reaction to her than she is with her own feelings and desires.

Often our journey through life begins with us looking outside of ourselves for identity, security, and happiness. When we finally begin to look INSIDE for these, we start making choices that honor and respect our true spirit.

For many people this is the most important part of their journey!

Now realize, people start on this path at different places and travel at different rates. Some people seem to be born with an inner confidence; they barely seem fazed by Outside Pressure. Others spend a lifetime and never find this inner peace and security.

RESPECT Respect is a two-way street, not a one-way lane. It is important to respect others, but it's also important to receive respect. Now you can't make or force others to be respectful, but you do choose how you treat yourself. When you respect yourself, not only do you make choices that honor you, but you also model how you expect to be treated. If you want others to respect you and your wishes, it's important that you respect yourself first. If you consistently give in to other people's pressure, you are not respecting yourself.

How can you expect others to respect you if you don't respect yourself?

Social Pressure

Social Pressure is Outside Pressure. It is the pressure that comes from society to act or not act in certain ways. This isn't all bad. Think about it.

Why do people stop talking during a movie after others turn around and look at them? Because of social pressure.

Why do people not pick their noses in public? Because of social pressure.

There is always going to be some pressure to adhere to group standards.

The most famous type of social pressure is Peer Pressure. People talk about Peer Pressure as if it is something that happens only to preteens and teens. But people can be influenced by social pressure/peer pressure their whole lives.

He who trims himself to suit everyone will soon whittle himself away.

Raymond Hull, Canadian Author (1919–1985)

A coworker is selling Girl Scout cookies for her daughter. Everyone is buying some. Then she approaches you. You really don't want the cookies but you buy them anyway. Why? Because others are watching and you are concerned about what they would think.

You are having a heated discussion with a friend and people are starting to look, so you suggest getting in the car to carry on the conversation. Why? You don't want to make a scene. You are worried about what other people might think.

All your friends had big parties for their children's birthdays. They keep asking what you are doing for your child's birthday. You don't want to appear cheap, or out of touch, or like an insensitive parent, so you plan a big party too.

But wait. Did you change your behavior because other people put pressure on you or because you put pressure on yourself? Was it Outside Pressure or Inside Pressure that primarily influenced your decision?

We often think of social pressure, especially peer pressure, as something that happens **TO US**—others putting pressure on us to act in certain ways. But the most important part of social pressure/peer pressure is the pressure we put on ourselves to fit in, not look foolish, or impress our peers.

The most important part of social pressure/peer pressure comes from INSIDE. It's Inside Pressure.

In truth, sometimes people do exert pressure, trying to influence our behavior, trying to get us to conform to THEIR standards or wishes, or trying to get us to act the way THEY WANT. They may judge and criticize us, or watch over our lives and think they know how we should be or act. Friends, family members, coworkers, employers, communities, organizations, advertisers, and political groups all may try to pressure us and influence our behavior at some time. And if we worry about these other people's opinions, we may alter our behavior to better fit their beliefs or wishes.

And peer pressure during preteen and teen years can be extremely strong for a variety of reasons:

◆   This is a period involving much change—change in bodies, change in interests, change in personal styles. Change is stressful and usually involves uncertainty and confusion, all of which makes us more susceptible to outside influences.

◆   We are social beings, we want to belong. We want to fit in and be liked by the people with whom we associate. And since teens primarily associate with other teens, this is the group they look to for acceptance and support. This is their society. And because teens often look to each other for this acceptance and support, they give this group more influence over them.

◆   Teens are in the process of moving from dependence to independence. They are beginning to separate from their parents and develop their own identities. Part of this process includes experimenting and testing out different styles. (Like test-driving a car to see if you want to buy it.) And where do teens find these different identities to test-drive? In their peers. So here again, they look to each other.

Remember, our journey through life often begins with us looking outside of ourselves for our identity. The preadult years are often an extremely stressful time in this journey as we experiment, question, and learn about ourselves and how we relate to others. The sooner we begin to look inside for our answers and the less we let outside influences alter our beliefs, feelings, and actions, the less we allow social pressure to affect us.

No matter what your age, if you do not worry about pleasing others or worry what they think about you, then your Inside Pressure is going to be low. If your Inside Pressure is low, then someone's Outside Pressure won't work.

Think of it like this.

You are 18 and two people are pushing at you to do what they want; one is your 12 brother and the other is a friend.

Your brother begs and then gets mad and says he doesn't like you anymore. He threatens to get you back if you don't do what he wants.

He is trying to use Outside Pressure. Does it work? Are you worried about what he thinks? Are you afraid he'll be mad? Probably not in the least. His Outside Pressure doesn't work because you feel little Inside Pressure to appease him.

But what happens when your friend pushes at you to do what they want? Do you feel pressure to please them? Are you worried what they think? How much Inside Pressure do you feel—probably a lot more than you did with your little brother.

> That you may retain your self-respct, it is better to displease the people by doing what you know is right, than to temporarily please them by doing what you know is wrong.
>
> *William J.H. Boetcker, American Religious Leader and Public Speaker (1873–1962)*

Which of these two would you most likely give into?

You see, Outside Pressure doesn't work without Inside Pressure.

QUESTIONS FOR YOU

*E*arlier you were asked, "Who can easily manipulate you?" and "Why do you find it hard to stand up to them?" Do your answers have anything to do with the pressure you put on yourself to impress them, please them, fit in, or not offend them, etc.?

Does it have anything to do with Inside Pressure?

? ?

Learning to Shut the Door

Think about a time when someone wanted you to do something you didn't want to do.

◆ Did you say "NO"? How strong was your "NO"?

◆ Did you hesitate, or waver, or just 'kind of' hint you didn't want to do what they wanted?

◆ Did you say "NO," and then give in after they applied pressure?

Maybe you told them you wanted time to think before you made your decision.

◆ Did they give you time, or did they keep pressuring and trying to persuade you?

◆ Did you listen to them, or did you firmly remind them that you wanted time to think?

When you tell someone "NO" in a firm way, you **SHUT THE DOOR**. You don't need to slam it shut (get loud or angry); just say it firmly ("NO, I don't want to.") and then keep it shut (stick with your answer).

If you hesitate, waver, or don't really give them an answer, then you leave the door open. Maybe you leave it open only a crack. But a crack is a crack. They see that little opening and think that if they just apply more pressure they can push that door open and get what they want.

So they try some manipulative tricks. They keep talking, bending the truth, begging, bribing, acting real nice, or involving others to increase the pressure. They may try to make you feel bad, guilty, sorry for them, or scared. They may even try force to 'make' you to do what they want.

Heck, even if you say "NO" (SHUT THE DOOR), they may still apply Outside Pressure in an attempt to get you to change your mind. They may call you names, say you are rude or inconsiderate, get mad at you, or say you don't care and you aren't a real friend. They may use any trick they think will work to get you to open the door and do what they want.

But wait; let's turn this around. Are they considering your wishes and feelings? Aren't they being rude and inconsiderate? Do they care about you? Are they being a good friend? Who are they thinking about?

And who are you thinking about? Do your thoughts create Inside Pressure? Are you afraid you might hurt their feelings or make them mad? Or maybe you are worried they will make fun of you or stop being your friend.

If this pressure works and they get you to change your mind and give in and do what they want, what did they learn about you?

We teach people how to treat us.

Remember: Outside Pressure doesn't work without Inside Pressure.

When you stick with your answer, others may get upset or mad because they aren't getting what they want. (So are they mad at you because you are an 'evil,' 'terrible' person, or are they really mad at you because they didn't get their way?) You may even lose some of these people as friends, even someone you thought was a 'special' friend. But if they like you only when you do what they want, were they really a 'true friend' to begin with?

True friends care about you. They respect your wishes and opinions and care about your feelings. So you feel comfortable and safe around true friends. Even if you have a difference or a conflict, you work it out.

But other so-called friends (false friends) care more about themselves than you, so they try to trick or manipulate you to get what they want. False friends can't be trusted. You feel unsure, uncomfortable, pressured, or on guard when you are around false friends.

So when you don't want to do something, learn to SHUT THE DOOR. With a firm voice say, "NO." Then keep the door closed (stick with your answer) no matter what tricks (begging, bribing, getting mad, etc.) the other person uses.

SHUTTING THE DOOR
HOW TO STAND UP FOR YOURSELF

1. Stand up tall and use a strong voice.

Try this: Let your shoulders drop, look down at the ground and weakly say, "I don't want to." Now put your shoulders back, look up and firmly state, "I don't want to." Which one sounds like you mean it? When you SHUT THE DOOR, make sure your body language and your tone of voice are strong.

2. State your position. Make it short and to the point. Use short definite statements to show you know exactly what you do and don't want.

You don't need to:

- ◆ Defend yourself or your position. "Well, I think this because of...." This is just your position. They don't have to agree with you. Just like you don't have to agree with them. There is nothing wrong with you having a different position.

- ◆ Make excuses. "I'm having a bad day."

- ◆ Give them a reason. "It's because...."

- ◆ Attack them. "Well, if you would have listened in the first place...."

- ◆ Argue with them or debate your position. The other person may try to get you to discuss the matter. But once you've made your decision, this isn't a discussion. This is your position.

So just state your position. "That's how I feel and that's what I want."

It's your life. It's your choice.

3. Stay Calm and Respectful (of yourself and others).

They may get upset and even try to get you upset. In fact, this may be part of their plan. As you get upset, your Thinking Brain shuts down, and they may be better able to manipulate you. So there is no need to be angry or emotional; just calmly and respectfully repeat your position.

4. Repeat, Repeat, Repeat your position if necessary. Just keep saying the same short statement over and over.

5. Remove yourself from the situation.

Stand

State

Stay Calm & Respectful

Repeat

Remove

If you are not sure how you feel, take time to think about it without pressure from them. If someone does pressure you, that is a sure sign that they are not considering your feelings. And if you give in, that is a sure sign that you aren't either.

Have you ever seen a teenager argue with their parents to let them do something, like go to a party? They push and push. If a parent says "maybe," the teenager twists it and says, "You said I could." They highlight the favorable points but cover up the unfavorable issues. They try to get the parent to defend their position and then argue

> **Our ultimate freedom is the right and power to decide how anybody or anything outside ourselves will affect us.**
>
> *Stephen Covey, Author and Speaker on Personal Development (1932–)*

against each of these defense statements. They sound rational and reasonable all to get what they want—to go to that party.

You know people who have done this to their parents. Maybe you even did this to your parents.

Learn to recognize it, because now we are talking about someone doing this to you.

You will encounter people who are adept at arguing and debating to get what they want. They are salespeople and they are selling their position. They will use any argument they think will work to make their sale.

DON'T GET TRICKED by these talking con artists. It's like they weave a verbal web around you to get you to weaken, question yourself, and GIVE IN and do what they want. They make their arguments sound reasonable as they try to convince you that you are wrong. They may twist your words and comments to strengthen their argument. Or they will use a statement you made against you. These people don't look evil. Often, they look like a friend; in fact they may be a friend.

What part of NO don't you understand?

But the whole purpose of their verbal trickery is to get what they want. DON'T GET TRICKED.

The safest way to avoid getting caught in their web is to make your statements short, stay calm, and keep repeating your position. You DO NOT have to give a reason for your position, no matter how angry they get or how hard they push. In fact, if you defend your position, it gives them something they can argue against. And remember, their arguments will often sound reasonable. So don't argue. Don't debate. Don't defend. Just state your position, stay calm and respectful, repeat your position if you need to, and if you feel yourself getting tangled, leave.

+ + YOUR RIGHTS

You have the right to:

1. Feel the way you feel.

2. Say "NO."

3. Change your mind.

4. Think differently from others.

5. Say, "I need time to think" and to think as long as you need (without pressure from them).

6. Say, "I don't know."

7. Offer no reasons or excuses to justify your decision.

Remember, if someone is pressuring you, they aren't thinking about you. They are thinking about themselves, what they want, and what they can do to get you to do what they want. So who is going to think about YOU?

The game of life is the game of boomerangs.
Our thoughts, deeds and words return to us sooner or later,
with astounding accuracy.

Florence Shinn, Author (1871–1940)

Happy he who learns to bear what he cannot change.

*Johann Friedrich von Schiller, German Poet, Philosopher,
and Historian (1759–1805)*

No one can make you feel inferior
without your consent.

*Eleanor Roosevelt, Former First Lady of the United States of America,
U.S. Diplomat and Reformer (1884–1962)*

Dwelling on the negative simply contributes to its power.

Shirley MacLaine, Actress (1934–)

Whether you think you can, or think you can't,
you're probably right.

Henry Ford, U.S. Automobile Industrialist (1863–1947)

Confidence is a habit that can be developed
by acting as if you already had the
confidence you desire to have.

*Brian Tracy, Business and Personal Management
Author and Speaker (1944–)*

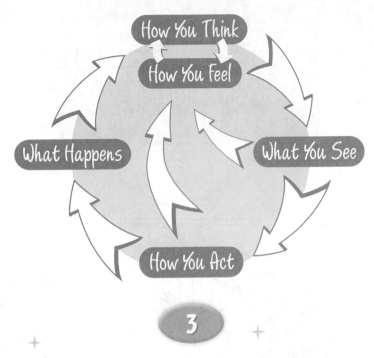

How You Think

How You Feel

What Happens

What You See

How You Act

3

Thoughts, Feelings, and Choicycles

Someone asks you to go to a concert. How do you answer them? Do you choose to go with them or do something else?

Someone calls you on the phone and starts yelling. How do you respond? What do you think? How do you feel?

Someone breaks the vase you inherited from your grandmother. What do you do?

Moment by moment you choose how you handle life.

No matter what happens

> Our greatest battles are that with our own minds.
>
> *Jameson Frank, Poet*

You CAN CHOOSE TO ACT MANY DIFFERENT WAYS.

How will Anne
choose to act?

If she thinks,
"Poor me. I always get left out,"
she might act like this:

If she thinks,
"Yeah right. Some friend you are,"
she might act like this:

If she thinks,
"That's okay,"
she might act like this:

If she thinks,
"Get Lost!!!"
she might act like this:

If she thinks,
"Yikes. No Way!!!
Those things scare me,"
she might act like this:

HOW YOU THINK IS THE MOST
IMPORTANT CHOICE YOU MAKE.

> How you THINK affects how you FEEL,
> how you SEE things, and how you ACT,
> which in turn affects WHAT HAPPENS to you.

It's a cycle:

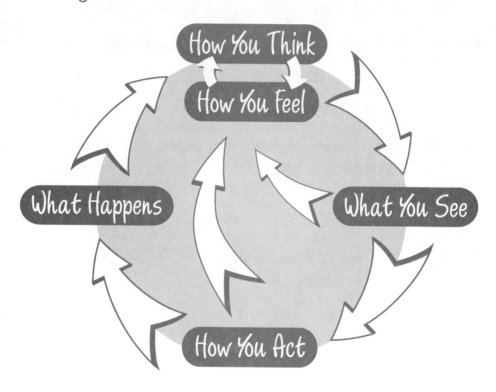

How you THINK affects everything.

You could have a positive 'feel good' cycle.

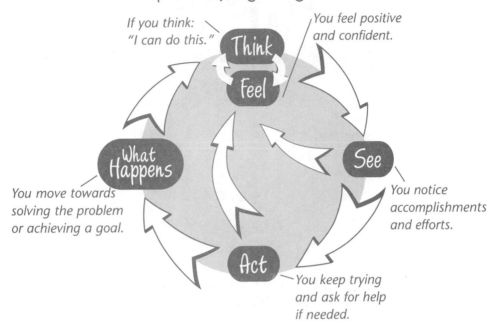

If you think: "I can do this."

You feel positive and confident.

Think

Feel

See

You notice accomplishments and efforts.

Act

You keep trying and ask for help if needed.

What Happens

You move towards solving the problem or achieving a goal.

You could have a negative 'feel bad' cycle.

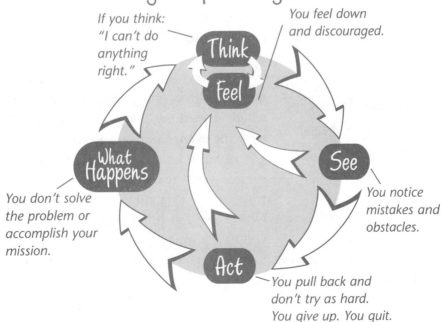

If you think: "I can't do anything right."

You feel down and discouraged.

Think

Feel

See

You notice mistakes and obstacles.

Act

You pull back and don't try as hard. You give up. You quit.

What Happens

You don't solve the problem or accomplish your mission.

It all starts with how you THINK.

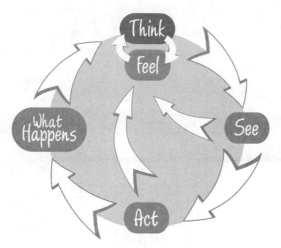

When something happens you often don't stop and ask, "How am I going to think about this event?" You just feel a certain way and react. It seems like you don't think at all; it's just a reaction.

That's because your thoughts are already there. You have developed habits (patterns) in the way you think about life.

If you have a habit of thinking clear, reasonable, peaceful thoughts, then when something happens you usually view the event from this perspective.

The meaning of things lies not in the things themselves but in our attitude towards them.

Antoine de Saint-Exupéry, French Writer and Aviator (1900–1944)

If you have a habit of thinking muddy, negative, stress producing thoughts, then when something happens you usually view the event from this perspective.

And since your thoughts are already there, you react quickly—seemingly without any thought.

The way you think is the biggest habit you have formed.

Your thoughts determine how you feel, see, and act, which all affect what happens.

Different Ways of Thinking

Think of your brain as a radio. You can listen to a station that plays Clear, Peaceful, Positive, Rational, and Optimistic Messages. Or you can listen to a station that plays Dark, Muddy, Negative, Critical, and Pessimistic Messages. And, of course, you can switch back and forth between these stations.

If you listen to the station that plays Clear, Peaceful, Positive, Rational, Optimistic Messages, you hear thoughts like:

I am important. People care. I can trust others. I belong. Life is good. I am thankful for what I have. I can handle this. Things will work out. I have talents. I will figure it out. Mistakes are just a part of life. I'll survive. The future looks bright.

But if you listen to the station that plays Dark, Muddy, Negative, Critical, Pessimistic Messages, you hear thoughts like:

Nobody cares. Nobody understands me. People always let me down. I don't belong. I'm not good enough. I never get what I want. Things aren't fair. This is terrible. Others are out to get me. People aren't fair or honest. I'm always messing up. Life is the pits.

The positive, up-beat thoughts are light and airy like feathers floating by, while the negative downer thoughts are more like heavy rocks and mud, they stick, stay with us longer, and weigh us down.

The station you listen to most affects the rest of your choicycle.

How you THINK affects how you FEEL.

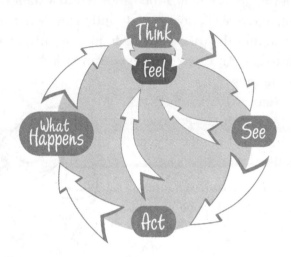

How you think affects how you feel. But your feelings also affect how you think. And it's even more complex than that.

To be perfectly honest, feelings came first. Long before you knew how to use words, you felt feelings. You felt safe or scared, loved or unloved, comfortable or uneasy. You just didn't know how to describe these feelings (and maybe you still don't).

As you got older, you learned to use words to think about life and describe your feelings. Now your thoughts play a large role in creating and supporting your feelings. Thoughts and feelings are so intertwined that they are hard to separate. Either way, your thoughts have a huge effect on your feelings, and your feelings have a huge effect on your thoughts.

Remember a time when you had a headache or felt sick. Weren't you a little crabby? When you are physically feeling down, your thoughts are often down too. The same is true when you are emotionally down.

If you feel unimportant, unwanted, unappreciated, or unloved, you are emotionally down, and your thoughts will reflect this too. In fact, it was your thoughts that labeled your feelings as unimportant, unwanted, unappreciated, or unloved.

Your thoughts and feelings cycle around and around, amongst themselves, and affect everything in your life.

Positive thoughts lead to positive feelings, and positive feelings lead to positive thoughts.

Negative thoughts lead to negative feelings, and negative feelings lead to negative thoughts.

You may say, "But look, I'm smiling and laughing and having fun; I must feel happy." And you may be at that moment. But, if you also complain and have negative thoughts, then at some level your feelings are negative too.

You see, your thoughts and feelings are like an onion. We can see the outer layer, but there are many more layers hidden underneath. So your outer surface may look happy and carefree, but underneath you could be unhappy or in turmoil. That's why someone who 'seems' happy may all of a sudden BLOW UP. Those angry feelings were there all along, just below the surface.

Or think of it like this: most people wear a mask. They present a social face to the world, but underneath they may feel very differently. They may wear different masks at different times with different people. And they may have many layers of masks. You would have to strip away all the masks to see how a person truly thinks and feels, including yourself.

These underneath layers are your true feelings, and they affect how you think and feel, and how you deal with life.

But remember, there are many layers of feelings underneath the outer layer. These underlying feelings can be confusing and complex. But no matter who you are, or what your situation, if you could dig through all the layers, release all your fears and worries and get to the core of you, you would relax and feel comfortable and learn to love and accept yourself.

What you THINK and FEEL affects what you SEE
because you tend to SEE what you THINK you will see.

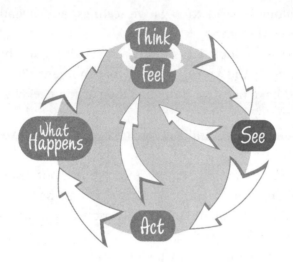

How you THINK and FEEL affects the way you view your world. It affects what you SEE, NOTICE, PAY ATTENTION TO, and FOCUS ON. It affects how you interpret what you SEE, NOTICE, PAY ATTENTION TO, and FOCUS ON. You tend to SEE what you THINK you will see, which then reinforces (validates, confirms) what you were thinking and feeling.

We don't see things as
they are, we see things
as we are.

Anais Nin, U.S. (French-born)
Author and Diarist
(1903–1977)

If you feel positive and think people will like you, then you tend to notice smiles and friendly gestures. If someone frowns, you may be concerned about them and ask what's wrong, but you don't take it personally. You don't jump to the conclusion that their frown has something to do with you.

If you feel negative and think people don't like you, then you tend to notice frowns and gestures you think are unfriendly. When someone frowns, you automatically think it must have something to do with you.

How you think and feel and what you see is a cycle too.

When we believe something, we look for things that agree with (validate, confirm) our thinking. So we often see what we are looking for. It becomes a self-fulfilling prophecy. We predict what will happen, and then we look for things to confirm our prediction.

Think about it.

If you are working on a project with a group, and you feel negative and think you are not being treated fairly, what type of things would you notice? How would you judge or interpret what you 'saw'?

Now, if instead you feel positive and aren't worried about fairness, what type of things would you notice? How would you judge or interpret what you 'saw'?

Have you ever heard someone say another person was rude? But you were there the whole time and you didn't think the other person was rude. The person who made this comment saw the event from their perspective, the way they thought, and only noticed actions or comments that confirmed their thinking. Now who is right?

> Our life is what our thoughts make it. A man will find that as he alters his thoughts toward things and other people, things and other people will alter towards him.
>
> *James Allen, British-born American Essayist, (1864–1912)*

Or have you ever heard someone complain that they weren't treated fairly when you didn't see it that way at all? They too saw the event from their perspective, the way they thought. And they noticed only the things that confirmed their thinking. Who is right?

You do that too.

But since you are thinking your thoughts, you think you are right. Others may not see things the way you see them.

People with dark, muddy thoughts tend to:

◆ look for and spotlight what's wrong, ignoring the good things in their lives;

◆ focus on what they don't have, rather than what they do have;

◆ look for things they THINK they NEED to be happy;

◆ focus on disappointments;

◆ look for things in the future to worry about;

◆ jump to negative conclusions as to what something means;

◆ take everything personally, and see another person's actions as being about them;

◆ keep score, noticing and remembering every inequity, every disappointment, and every hurt.

Because people with dark, muddy thoughts notice, focus on, and remember the things they don't like, they are weighed down with unhappy, negative thoughts. Negative thoughts and feelings feel heavy.

People with clear, positive thoughts tend to:

◆ focus on the good things and the possibilities in their lives;

◆ focus on what they have and are thankful;

◆ see something they want as something they WANT, not something they NEED;

◆ enjoy life today rather than review past disappointments or get stuck worrying about all the possibilities in the future;

◆ see multiple interpretations and stay focused on their own actions rather than worry about what others are thinking or doing;

◆ see other people as separate individuals with their own problems and moods, unrelated to them;

◆ be too busy enjoying life rather than spending time keeping score.

And because people with clear, positive thoughts mostly notice and focus on the things they like, they aren't weighed down by all those negative thoughts. Their moods are lighter and freer.

How you THINK, FEEL, and SEE affects how you ACT.

When you THINK and FEEL positive and peaceful you tend to:

◆ stay calm and relaxed;
◆ be flexible and open to suggestions and other possibilities;
◆ accept and even ask for help;
◆ stay upbeat and optimistic;
◆ view difficult problems as challenges;
◆ take risks;
◆ do your best and care.

And around others you tend to:

◆ smile and act friendly, welcoming, and respectful;
◆ be accepting and positive;
◆ be supportive and complimentary;
◆ forgive and move on;
◆ include them and show you care;
◆ show interest in them, share, listen;
◆ compromise and cooperate rather than compete;
◆ accept responsibility for your actions and apologize when it's appropriate.

When you THINK and FEEL negative and muddy you tend to:

◆ get upset, frustrated, and impatient;
◆ close your mind to other options and opinions;
◆ try to do everything yourself (others don't do it right);
◆ act like a martyr or a victim;
◆ criticize and pick things apart;
◆ avoid taking risks;
◆ ACT like you don't care, like it's not important.

And around others you tend to:

◆ frown, be distant and withdrawn, unfriendly, or rude;
◆ get angry or upset easily;
◆ complain, criticize, and sulk;
◆ say and do hurtful things (feel the need to get back at others—retaliate);
◆ exclude others and act superior;
◆ focus mainly on yourself and your wants;
◆ demand that things go your way;
◆ not listen;
◆ compete, not cooperate;
◆ blame someone or something when things don't go the way you want.

How you act also affects how you think and feel. When you smile and sing you tend to feel upbeat. When you frown and complain you drag yourself down.

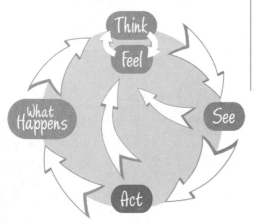

How you ACT affects WHAT HAPPENS.

Look at the lists of the ways people could act on the previous page.

Which person might try something new and difficult, and therefore learn something that might be helpful to them now or in the future?

Which person might give up more easily?

Which person might be better able to think more clearly?

Which person might get angry or impatient?

Which person might face a problem and therefore have a chance to solve it?

Which person might avoid a problem so it never gets resolved?

Which person might risk proposing a novel idea, even if others might laugh?

Now, which person would you rather work with on a project?

If you were to make a mistake, which person would probably treat you better?

How you act affects how others act towards you. Some actions attract people and some actions push people away.

Your actions affect how others act towards you, but they don't cause other people's actions. Their actions are a result of their own thoughts.

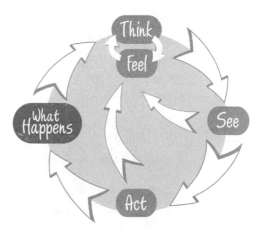

You are today where your thoughts have brought you;
you will be tomorrow where your thoughts take you.

James Lane Allen, Author (1849–1925)

You are in control of your life.
You are what you are because of the
conscious and subconscious choices you have made.

Barbara Hall, Writer and Producer (1961–)

A happy person is not a person in a certain set of circumstances,
but rather a person with a certain set of attitudes.

Hugh Downs, Television Host (1921–)

You can make more friends in two months by becoming
interested in other people than you can in two years
by trying to get other people interested in you.

Dale Carnegie, Author and Speaker on Personality Development (1888–1955)

Thoughts lead on to purposes; purposes go forth in action;
actions form habits; habits decide character;
and character fixes our destiny.

Tyron Edwards, New England Preacher (1809–1894)

Change your thoughts and you change your world.

Norman Vincent Peale, Clergyman and Author (1898–1993)

4

Adjusting Your
Personal Radio Station

(Changing Your Thoughts)

What thought station do you mostly tune into—the positive, accepting, optimistic station or the negative, critical, pessimistic station? **And even more important, if you don't like the station you tune into, can you change stations?**

We all have negative thoughts at times. It's part of being human. But you can learn to question, adjust, and alter your thinking. You can develop patterns to help you primarily tune into the positive station and learn how to change stations when you do find yourself on the negative station.

The most important thing to remember about your thoughts is that they are YOUR THOUGHTS. You created them.

Just because you THINK something doesn't mean it's true.

We often just accept our thoughts and act as if they are proven facts. But, didn't we just make them up in our head?

There are several problems with our thinking.

First, most of the time our minds are not entirely in our control. You are at work, or in a class, or at dinner, and all of a sudden you realize that your mind is somewhere else. In fact it's been a lot of 'somewhere elses.' In a very short time, your thoughts have traveled all over the place, and now you are thinking about a new song you heard, or something you saw, or possible (or impossible) things that could happen. How did your thoughts end up there? You didn't consciously decide to think about all those things; it just happened.

Your mind seems to have a 'mind' of its own. It goes places on its own that you don't seem to control.

How many times have you tried to stop yourself from thinking a thought, singing a song, replaying a memory, or worrying about a problem? You say to yourself, "Stop it. Stop thinking, singing, worrying." Well, did it work? Were you able to stop? Maybe for a short time, but pretty soon you're back to thinking, singing, worrying again. How did you get back there? Who is in control here—you or your mind?

Second, not only does our mind travel all over the place, but look where it goes. We often don't just enjoy our moments. We analyze, rehash, judge, and re-create events in our life. We jump to conclusions about what every little look, comment, or stumble means. Like a cow chewing its cud, we go over and over and over the same thoughts in our heads. Or we imagine the future, creating different scenes and events as we hope they will be. And we create the same scene again and again. And while we relive or dream about our lives, we miss what is happening right now. We relive the past and think or worry about the future, and we miss the present.

Third, our minds often focus on the negative. Look—200 good things could happen in a day, but lying in bed late at night what do you think about…those good things or the one or two (or three or four) stumbles, mistakes, or mishaps? What about those wonderful things? We often pick ourselves and our lives apart, and while we are at it, we pick apart others too.

But wait. Who controls our thoughts? Can't we choose to think differently? If we criticize and condemn ourselves or others, who created this judgment?

Just because we think those thoughts doesn't make them true.

Our thoughts are just that— our thoughts. We created them in our own brains. So if your thoughts aren't pleasant, positive, and supportive, question them and learn to create new ones that are.

Remember, the same brain you use to solve problems can also create problems. If you think negative thoughts, you create unhappiness for yourself.

The Story of Your Life

Jeremy lives in an apartment with his mom and three younger siblings. He had a job that helped pay some of the bills, but the shop closed and now he's looking for a new job. He also just started a commercial design class at a local college.

So what is Jeremy's story?
He could tell it like this:

"My mom is doing the best she can and I'm helping her. I'll get another job. It will work out. Maybe the people at the college can help. I'm really looking forward to the class. I'm going to keep taking classes so someday I can get a job that pays well."

Or he could tell it like this:

"Man, nothing works out. Now what am I going to do? I've got no job. I have to live here with my mom and the kids. They don't help enough. And now I'm taking this class. What's it going to do for me? I'm working harder than everyone else. It's not fair."

Whichever story Jeremy decides to tell reflects his perception of his reality. It affects how he feels, how he sees things, and how he acts, which then affects what happens to him. (It's the Choicycle.) And it all starts with the story he decides to tell about his life.

We are always creating stories about our lives. Stories about what has happened, what is going to happen, what we wish would happen. Our minds go over and over stories and different scenarios, all simply created in our heads.

If we are walking and someone hurries past us and we think they are racing us, this becomes our story. This may be true, but they also could just be thinking of something and in a hurry. So could that be our story too?

When we try something and it doesn't work out, we could think, "I'm always a screw-up," or "Well, that didn't work. What's next?"

So which one would become your story?

We may even create multiple stories.

When someone frowns, we could think, "Why are they upset at me? I wonder if they heard me wrong? What if they thought I cut in? Maybe they are upset because I yelled at them from across the street? Maybe…."

Oh, the places our minds travel.

Any of this may be true, but they also could be thinking of something they forgot or what they need to do when they get home. They could be confused by a problem they have or thinking about something someone said to them earlier, or remembering a conversation they overheard, or...well, you get the picture.

If we have a tendency to have negative thoughts, our stories will have a negative twist.

The other person is out to get me...I'm really not as good as people think I am...if they only knew what I was really like, they wouldn't like me...other people think they are better than I am...there is something wrong with me...and on and on.

All these are possible stories we can make up about ourselves. And where are these stories? IN OUR HEADS.

Just because we think these thoughts, does that make them true?

Can't we just create a different story in our heads?

And why do we have to have a story anyway?

The other person frowned. Big deal. Leave it at that. Don't try to figure it out. Heck, it's hard enough just figuring ourselves out; don't even try to figure out someone else.

How you choose to think determines the life you lead.

? ? QUESTIONS FOR YOU

Think about your life.

Create a negative story about it.

Now create a positive story.

Which story is true?

They both are, depending on your perception.

Which story will lead towards happiness and success?

And which story will lead towards disappointment and frustration?

That's what's really important.

Now break your life down into little stories. For each of the following, tell a negative story, then a positive story. If you normally have a positive attitude, this may be difficult to do. But try.

- ◆ your family
- ◆ a couple of your friends
- ◆ something you recently tried
- ◆ your home
- ◆ your possessions
- ◆ your talents
- ◆ your day so far
- ◆ the rest of the day to come

Which stories help make your life better?

You choose how you tell the story of your life, the little stories and the big story. And remember, the little stories are just chapters in your life. Little stories add up to form the big story.

? ?

Out of Control Thoughts

The ability to create your own story and change your perception of your life is one of the greatest abilities you have. Because no matter what happens, you decide how you will view it. You have the power to choose the story you tell.

Many people don't recognize they have a choice. They think their happiness or their misery is based entirely upon what happens to them. But to think you have no choice is like being a puppet. People and events control you. You have no choice. You are helpless, powerless, and weak. You just react to whatever comes your way.

To recognize that you have the ability to choose feels powerful. You are free and in charge. And you can feel this way no matter what your circumstances. Because you create the stories you tell yourself.

In some ways your brain works against you. Your brain was developed to protect you. It was wired so you could react quickly to threatening events. In more primitive times, the threats were physical. But for today's humans with our Thinking Brain, threats can come from our thoughts about anything—something in the newspaper, the way someone looked at us, a comment, our interpretation, bills, worries, etc. The moment a threat is perceived, our brain kicks into action. But which brain kicks into action? Our Survival Brain, which just reacts in a fight-or-flight response? Our Emotional Brain, with its memory of threats and fears, which then releases stress hormones helping us to be quicker and stronger? Or our Thinking Brain, which can evaluate the threat, dismiss it, or analyze it, and develop appropriate actions?

Well, when we perceive a threat, the Survival Brain and the Emotional Brain react first. That's just the way our brains developed over time.

So our Survival Brain and our Emotional Brain can be off and running with a worry before the Thinking Brain kicks into gear. In fact, they may hijack the Thinking Brain and now your mind spins out of control with troublesome, worrying thoughts before you truly use your Thinking Brain to evaluate the situation and say, "Wait a minute. There's nothing to worry about here."

When has that happened to you? Your mind goes spinning off, worrying about something. Then all of a sudden you catch yourself, realize that there is nothing to worry about or that your worries have gotten out of control, and try to calm yourself down. The problem is sometimes your mind has gained so much steam, and you are so caught up in your thoughts, that it just keeps running totally out of control. You are left thinking those thoughts over and over, and now they are running your life. You totally discount or don't listen to the rational part of your Thinking Brain.

It's like a snowball rolling down a mountain, gaining speed and energy as it goes. What started as a little thought often grows and

expands into other areas. Then your thoughts are out of control and it's difficult to stop them. They just sweep you up and carry you with them.

But the Thinking Brain has power too. You just have to learn how to use it.

First, it has the power to stop these thoughts before they get rolling. The moment you start thinking a negative, worrisome thought, STOP yourself. Tell yourself, "Don't go there." Throw that thought away. Don't even give it a chance to form.

Put a physical action with this. Tap yourself on the wrist or head. Act like you are throwing or flipping the thought away. Do whatever works to help you stop yourself and dismiss this thought.

Remember, the best time to catch and release these thoughts is when you first start to think them—before they gain momentum.

List some negative or worrisome thoughts you have repeated over and over in the past. Most of these aren't new. You've thought them many times before. But now that you've got the list, you can start noticing when they crop up. And as soon as they do, throw them away. Don't even let them start to form.

Wishes and thoughts can snowball into cravings and obsessions. All sorts of ideas can snowball on you if you allow yourself to keep thinking them.

"I like that chocolate. I really would like to get some, but I always eat too much. This time I won't. I'll just eat one piece a day. I'll control myself.... It sure is good. Well, maybe I'll eat two pieces...or three...."

It's much easier to stop this thought (and action) in the beginning before you allow it to snowball.

"I like that chocolate. Stop. I'm not going there. Keep on moving. I don't need to get it. Let's see, what else do I need to do today?"

Try not to give it a second thought, because a second thought often leads to a third, fourth, fifth...100th thought.

> Find something to be happy about every day, and every hour, even if only for a few minutes, and if possible moment-to-moment.
> This is the easiest and best protection you can have.
>
> *Gregg Braden,*
> *Scientist and Author (1956–)*

Second, use the power of your Thinking Brain. Question your thoughts. Do they really make sense? Is the story you are telling yourself really true? Can you tell another story? What makes one story more true than the other? Aren't both just stories you made up in your own head?

There are many different ways to question your thoughts. Here is a set of questions from a program called "The Work," developed by Byron Katie.

If you think "I'm so dumb," or "I'm so ugly," or "Nobody likes me," ask yourself these questions:

Q: *Is this true?*
A: Am I really dumb or ugly? Is it true that NOBODY likes me?

Q: *Can I ABSOLUTELY know that it's true?*
A: When we are upset and our thoughts get out of control, we tend to exaggerate and believe our thoughts are 'the truth.' We claim something is true when really we don't absolutely know it is true. So do you absolutely know? And if you are exaggerating, how does that help?

Q: *How do I react when I believe this thought?*
A: Do I skip around and act happy or do I sulk. Do I feel warm and fuzzy or sad, down, and unimportant?

Q: *Who would I be without this thought?*
A: I would be happier and calmer. I'd like myself more and I would notice the people who liked me.

So, if with these thoughts (which you created in your head) you feel upset and without these thoughts (which you created in your head) you feel fine, light, happy, hopeful, and important…where is the problem? (Hint: It's in the thoughts—the stories created in your head.)

MORE EXAMPLES

Thought: It's not fair. I always get the worst assignment. It should be fair.

Q: *Is this true?*
A: Well, most of the time.

Q: *Can you absolutely know that this is true?*
A: Well, no.

Q: *How do you react when you believe this thought?*
A: I'm angry and I don't even want to work on the project. I fight it. I grumble and complain.

Q: *Who would you be without this thought?*
A: I'd be happier. I'd probably just work and do the best I could. I wouldn't complain. I'd probably do a better job. I'd be more fun to be with.

So with this thought—miserable. Without this thought—happier and more productive. Where is the problem? Is your misery coming from the assignment or from your negative story about the assignment? And where is that story? You created it in your own head.

Thought: Look! I messed up again. I never do anything right.

Q: *Is this true?*
A: Well, most of the time.

Q: *Can you absolutely know that it's true?*
A: Well, no. Not absolutely.

(continues on next page)

(continued from previous page)

Q: *How do you react when you believe this thought?*
A: I feel useless and incompetent. I don't even like myself.

Q: *Who would you be without this thought?*
A: I'd be more confident. I'd feel better about myself and notice things I did well. I'd like myself.

So with this thought—depressed. Without this thought—optimistic. So what is causing your problem, messing up or your judgmental thought about messing up? And where is the thought? Who created it?

Thought: They don't like me.

Q: *Is this true?*
A: Well, they yelled at me.

Q: *Can you absolutely know that this is true?*
A: Well, I think so.

Q: *But can you absolutely know that this is true?*
A: Well, no. I can't absolutely know because I can't read their minds.

Q: *How do you react when you believe this thought?*
A: I'm angry. I do things to get back at them.

Q: *Who would you be without this thought?*
A: I would be calmer. I wouldn't worry about them so much. And if they yelled, I'd just think they were in a bad mood. It reflects their mood and their thoughts. I'd be friendlier. I'd feel better. I wouldn't let them ruin my mood. I'd be happier.

So with this thought—angry and hurt. Without this thought—happy and friendlier. So how could they be the problem? Where is the thought?

What negative thoughts/stories cause you pain?

What negative thoughts/stories would you let go?

Now use both hands to roll these thoughts into a ball. Put them in one hand. Hold them tight. Now hold out this fist, then open it, and just imagine dropping these thoughts.

Now you try these questions on one of your negative thoughts.

What is your negative thought?

Q: Is this true?

Q: Can you absolutely know that this is true?

Q: How do you react when you believe this thought?

Q: Who would you be without this thought?

So with this thought you feel…

And without this thought…

So where is the problem?

Notice the stories you tell yourself, and when you make up a story that causes you pain, drop the story and create a new one.

It's all in your mind anyway.

Use your mind to solve problems, not create them.

(This is just an introduction to Byron Katie's The Work. *There are additional components to this program. For more information, visit www.byronkatie.com).*

Accepting Life–Playing the Hand You Were Dealt

So what kind of hand did you get dealt in life? Do you like all your cards? Probably not. Each of us has some cards we would rather not have. Maybe you got a card that says, "Your older sister torments you." Or, "Your best friend turns against you." Or, "You have a flat tire and miss an important meeting." Or maybe, "Your mother drinks too much." Or, "Your special someone left."

You really don't want these cards, so can't you just get rid of them? Snap your fingers and make them disappear and have your life be the way you want?

Oh–that doesn't work.

Well how about if you get real angry, or complain, or throw a fit. Maybe that will make those difficult cards disappear.

Good luck.

Often when things don't go the way we want, we get upset and we fight it. We fight life. We fight reality.

We say, "I don't want this in my life. I want things to be the way I want them to be." We get angry. "This shouldn't have happened to me!"

Throughout our lives we have fought many things. We have gotten angry at the weather, the political scene, the traffic, the way others treated us, our financial situation, the results of a game, the results of a test. We have fought the way other people act, even the way certain members of our family act. We have gotten angry at our size, our shape, our looks, our performance. We've been angry about things in the past or about problems we are facing right now. And does this change things?

Do our problems disappear because we are upset? Do we ever win these battles?

If it's raining and you cancel your plans, you may be disappointed. But if you mope around complaining, what good does that do? Will it make the rain go away? Who is hurt the most by your moping?

You are late and you are stuck in traffic. Does complaining or getting angry help? Does it make the traffic move faster? Does it make your life better? And if you get angry and fight this, can you win this battle?

The guy you like asked someone else out. That's what happened. If you sit around complaining and feeling sorry for yourself, will that change anything? Or will it just make you miserable? And if you're miserable, are you fun to be with? Let it go. Move on. If you don't, you could be missing out on having a good time doing something else. You could even miss out on meeting someone else who you might really like. Besides, people are attracted to positive people. If you're miserable, who will you attract?

Reality is reality. The hand you were dealt is the hand you were dealt. No matter how upset you get and how much you yell and complain, it is still there. So what good are you doing yourself by getting upset?

When you fight what is—when you fight reality—YOU LOSE. You lose because reality isn't going to change. What you have power over is your attitude and your actions. You have power over the way you view and play your hand. And the way you play your cards influences the present and the future.

You don't like that you are poor and can't buy what you want. Is feeling embarrassed and being upset going to change anything? Do what you can, take actions to improve your life but for right now accept what you have and learn to be happy. Besides, what other choice do you have? Be miserable? And how does that make your present or future better?

When things don't go the way you want, definitely take action where you can, but drop the drama around it. Drama just creates negative energy.

Ask yourself:

How can I play this hand to make the best out of it?

Can I do anything? Talk to someone? Change anything?

If the answer is yes, then do it.

If the answer is no, then play the best you can with the cards you were dealt and move on.

Recognize what you can control. You can control yourself, your words, your actions, your thoughts, and your feelings. But also recognize what is out of your control. You don't control anything or anyone outside of you, which includes others (friends, parents, siblings), the world, and the outcome of events.

So your parents yell all the time. You don't like to hear them yell. In fact, you hate it. And what good does hating it do? Does it make them stop? Does it make your life better or worse? It's already unpleasant—your being upset only adds to the unpleasantness. Accept the fact that you have parents who yell. Stop focusing on them, and instead focus on something else in your life, something more positive, something you do control.

You could create a life story that focuses on their yelling and how much you hate it. Or your story could focus on other positive things in your life. It's your story. Which one would you rather tell?

"But," you may say, "can't I try to do something to get them to stop yelling?" Of course you can try. You can talk to them. Tell them how you feel. But remember, their actions are based on their thoughts and feelings. You don't control this—they do. So if you tell them how you feel and they choose to change, GREAT. But if they don't, focus on what you can do to make YOUR life better. Get involved in some activities that keep you busy. Focus on the positives in your life.

Start thinking of life like this:

These are my parents and I'll make the best of it. Why?
Because these are the parents I have. And if I fight what I have, I'm fighting reality. That doesn't change what is; it only makes me miserable. What can I learn from this to make my life better? Besides, I don't have to live with them forever.

◆ ◆ ◆

I didn't get the position I wanted, but I can live with that. Why?
Because that's what happened and what good would it do me to fight it? Instead, I'll focus on what I can do next.

When you focus on what you can do, you move forward instead of wallowing in misery. And when you move forward, good things often happen.

Now you try it:

Think of something you don't like in your life.

Now, look for the ways you are fighting it.

What are you saying? What is your story?

How do you feel with this story?

Picture yourself fighting it.

Now say:

This is the way life is and I'll make the best of it. Why?

Because this is what is.

Now create a different story.

How does that feel?

You don't get to choose the cards life places in your hand. But you do get to choose how you play them. And how you play your cards influences the new cards you are dealt. Your attitude and actions determine the direction you go in life.

> **Life is not holding a good hand. Life is playing a poor hand well.**
>
> *Danish Proverb*

But it's important to realize you never have total control. No matter what you do, life could deal you new difficult cards. And when this happens, you have new choices to make. And then those choices influence what happens next. It's always going to be that way. Life deals you a card and you choose how to play that card. And how you choose to play the card influences some of the new cards you are dealt.

✦ ✦ SO HOW ARE YOU PLAYING YOUR CARDS?

Are you fighting them? Are you fighting life?

Learn to change what you can, and then accept the rest.

You can change which friends you spend time with.

You can change your effort.

You can change what you do and how you act.

And most important...you can change your attitude.

No matter what your situation, happiness is within your reach—if you play your cards right.

Focus on What You Want

When you focus on how sad you are, your sadness grows.

When you focus on what you don't like, what you don't like takes a more prominent role in your life.

When you focus on how mean someone is, you notice all the things that person does that you don't like.

What you focus on grows simply because you focus on it.

So to get better, instead of focusing on what you do wrong, focus on what you do right.

To have more, instead of focusing on what you don't have, focus on what you do have.

To have a more positive experience, instead of focusing on eliminating the negative, focus on increasing the positive.

To be happier, instead of focusing on things you don't like, focus on things you do like.

It's all a matter of where you turn your attention. Because what you focus on grows.

Opportunity is sometimes hard to recognize
if you're only looking for a lucky break.

Monte Crane, Writer and Editor (1911–)

Things do not change; we change.

Henry David Thoreau, American Author, Poet, and Philosopher (1817–1862)

The better a man is, the more mistakes he will make,
for the more things he will try.
I would never promote into a top level job a man
who was not making mistakes.... He is sure to be mediocre.

Peter F. Drucker, U.S. (Austrian-born)
Business Management Professor and Author (1909–2005)

The greatest mistake you can make in life
is to be afraid of making one.

Elbert Hubbard, Author, Publisher, and Lecturer (1856–1915)

I'm a great believer in luck,
and I find the harder I work the more I have of it.

Thomas Jefferson, Third President of the
United States of America (1743–1826)

They always say time changes things,
but you actually have to change them yourself.

Andy Warhol, Artist (1928–1987)

5

Get Real–Be Sensible

When you think about yourself and your life, get real, be sensible.

◆ You don't HAVE TO have that job. You may really want it and your life may be easier if you have it, but you will continue living if you don't get it.

◆ Not EVERYONE will like you. That is just a fact of life, and it's true for every one of us.

◆ You won't ALWAYS be the best. There may always be someone better.

◆ Your life WON'T BE RUINED if you mess up. You may be inconvenienced and may have a difficult time for a while, but your life will go on.

◆ If that special someone doesn't like you, YOU WILL LIVE. Very few people die from a broken heart.

These are realities of life.

73

In truth, we create most of our unhappiness by **EXAGGERATING**,

"Life is NEVER fair."

Or having **unrealistic EXPECTATIONS**,

"I expect life to ALWAYS be fair."

Or **DEMANDING** that life (events and people) be the way we want them to be,

"Life SHOULD BE fair (especially for me)."

We cause our own pain by thinking irrational thoughts.

Exaggerating or Blowing Things out of Proportion

When we exaggerate, we turn minor issues into major problems, or we make major problems seem even bigger. These problems now take up more time, energy, and space in our lives.

"I didn't get what I wanted," becomes
"I NEVER get what I want!"

"I messed up," becomes
"I ALWAYS mess up!"

"I don't like it," becomes "I HATE it!"

"This is too bad," becomes
"This is TERRIBLE!"

"I'm unhappy," becomes
"I'll never be happy!"

Exaggerations are overblown versions of the truth—or at least what we want to see as the truth.

When we say that things ALWAYS or NEVER happen, or that EVERY-BODY or NOBODY does something, we have greatly overestimated our knowledge about life and all mankind.

When we speak as though the world is coming to an end ("the sky is falling...this is devastating...I can't go on"), we make a problem appear bigger and more overwhelming. The bigger we make a problem appear, the more it blocks our view. We can't see around the problem to find happiness or even see a future. But both are there.

Think back. You have handled problems in the past, and you can handle this one too, no matter how big it seems. You start by taking one small step at a time.

How does it help you to exaggerate? What good does this do? Does it lead to a positive thought cycle or a negative thought cycle?

When you find yourself exaggerating, stop and question your thinking.

Q: Is this true?

Q: Can I absolutely know that this is true?

Q: How do I react when I believe this thought?

Q: Who would I be without this thought?

Exaggerations don't help.

Unrealistic Expectations

Dream and plan and work, but be careful about setting expectations. When you expect something wonderful to happen and it doesn't, you may be greatly disappointed. And when your expectations are unrealistic, you will be disappointed more often. Be realistic about yourself and life. You won't always be first. You won't always get what you want. Life won't always be fair. These are just realities, and to expect anything different sets you up for unnecessary disappointments.

In fact, when we 'expect' certain wonderful things to happen, we are essentially demanding that life go the way we want. And demanding is what causes us trouble.

Making Demands of Life–'Musty' Thinking

We all have wants in life. We want to do well, win a contest, get a certain job, find our soul mate, etc. We want others to act a certain way, agree with us, like us, and like what we like. We want life to be fair and full of opportunities. All of this would make our lives easier. But just because we want something (or even expect it) doesn't mean it HAS TO happen. Life just goes the way it goes. We don't control it. We control our choices, our thoughts, and our actions, but we don't control other people and their choices, and we don't control what the world places on our plate.

When we start demanding that life go the way we want, we create problems for ourselves.

When we use the words MUST, MUSTN'T, SHOULD, SHOULDN'T, HAVE TO, or NEED TO, we turn our wishes, preferences, and requests into DEMANDS.

We DEMAND that things be the way we want them to be.

- ◆ I MUST do well.
- ◆ They MUST like me.
- ◆ I SHOULDN'T make mistakes.
- ◆ They SHOULDN'T act that way.
- ◆ I SHOULDN'T be upset.
- ◆ Life MUST be fair (especially for me).
- ◆ I HAVE TO have an answer.
- ◆ They HAVE TO respect me.
- ◆ I NEED TO be skinnier, better, wiser, healthier.

◆ I NEED TO get into that school or get that job.

◆ You NEED TO listen to me.

By DEMANDING, we act as though we are in charge of the entire world and that life has to be the way we want it to be, OR ELSE!

Or else what?

The sky will fall...the universe will dissolve...life won't go on? Get real. The universe doesn't revolve around you. You don't control what life brings to your plate. You aren't in charge here. You control only how you deal with it—your attitude and your behavior.

Now go back through this list of demands, and after each statement ask yourself, "Why?"

◆ Things MUST be the way I want them to be. Why?

◆ I MUST do well. Why?

Why does it have to be the way you want it to be?

It would be nice, but why does it HAVE TO be the way you want?

Demanding that life be the way we want creates problems in our lives. When we prefer that things go a certain way and they don't, we may be upset and disappointed. But when we demand that things go a certain way and they don't, our feelings are more intense. We now see it as terrible, awful, shameful, unbearable, horrible, appalling, and dreadful, and we feel angry, depressed, or filled with self-pity.

This shift in intensity is not caused by the event. It is caused by our own demanding thoughts about the event.

Dr. Michael R. Edelstein, a nationally acclaimed psychologist, speaker, and author calls this type of irrational thinking 'MUSTY' thinking. In his book (written with David Ramsay Steele) *Three Minute Therapy: Change Your Thinking, Change Your Life* (http://www.three-minutetherapy.com), he suggests that irrational thinking is at the root of most emotional turmoil. He then repeatedly shows how to question and argue against such irrational beliefs.

Irrational, demanding, musty thinking only makes your problem bigger and more difficult to handle, resolve, or even accept. Irrational, demanding, musty thinking makes your life harder.

Learn to accept and work with the realities of life.

Here are some basic realities of life:

Realities About You

You are not perfect; you are just perfectly human.

You will make mistakes. You will head in wrong directions. You will at some point say the wrong thing at the wrong time. You may try your hardest and still stumble. That's life.

Someone once said, "If I try and fail, I will be a failure."

But the real question is, "If you don't try, what are you?"

And remember, the most important part of making mistakes is how you handle them and what you learn. Each mistake is an opportunity to learn and grow. If you don't learn from your mistakes, you will keep repeating them.

*Here are some **musty thoughts** related to this: "I must be perfect." "I must not make a mistake." "I must always do things the 'right' way."*

You will be good at some things and not as good at others.

Be realistic and honest about your strengths and talents. There are areas where you will excel, and there are areas where you won't. Not all of us are cut out to be doctors or poets. Try things, and if you don't succeed at first, try them again at a later date. Explore to find your talents. If you aren't willing to risk failing, you may not even attempt something that is one of your talents. In general, you will do best when you focus on your strengths. Focusing on your struggles usually just leads to more struggles.

Musty thoughts: *"I must do well at everything." "I must succeed in the areas I choose."*

You are a work in progress.

You will develop strengths and talents throughout your life. So don't worry if you haven't a clue where you are headed right now, no matter what your age. Just accept where you are, continue to move forward, and trust that you will find your direction as you go along.

◆ Grandma Moses (Anna Mary Robertson Moses) didn't start painting until she was in her 70s. She painted more than 1,000 paintings before she died at the age of 101.

◆ I know a man who was relatively shy growing up and hated to speak in front of groups. He is now in his 50s and is an excellent public speaker.

◆ When I was 28, if you had told me I was going to 'grow up' to write books, I would have said you were crazy. Well, I too, am in my 50s and this is my fifth book.

You see, life is a marathon, not a sprint. Some people start out fast and then fade. Others start at the back of the pack, but they keep going one step at a time, and somewhere down the line, they finish. But the marathon of life doesn't have just one winner. Anyone who keeps going and making progress is a winner. So be a winner.

Life evolves one step at a time, one choice at a time. Be patient...and keep moving.

Musty thoughts: *"I must know what my talents are now." "I must figure out my life now before I can move forward."*

Big goals are achieved one step at a time.

Some problems and goals seem overwhelming; it seems as if you would have to do or change so much to overcome or achieve them. Instead of focusing on how big a problem is, focus on small steps you can

take. Even tiny steps add up. What can you do in the next week, the next day, the next hour?

One of my favorite books as a child was *The Big Jump* by Benjamin Elkin. In it, people tried to get to the top of a castle by making one big jump. None of them succeeded. But one boy realized that the way to make it to the top was by making many little jumps/steps.

So start climbing today.

Musty thoughts: *"I must not have big problems." "Life should be easier." "I must have what I want NOW!" "It shouldn't take me so long."*

There is no formula for success

People often think, "If I do X, Y, and Z then I should get what I want." They think that if they work hard enough and jump through all the necessary hoops they will get into the 'right' school, get the 'right' job, advance in their career, find their 'perfect' partner, make a lot of money, and be successful. Even a popular saying suggests, "If you try hard enough you can achieve anything." This isn't necessarily true.

> For peace of mind, we need to resign as general manager of the universe.
>
> *Larry Eisenburg*

Hard work and proper planning will suffice in many situations. But there are no guarantees! You could make all the 'right' moves, schmooze all the 'right' people, get all the 'right' training, and still not get what you want.

You can't predict or control life, and there are no guarantees that your efforts will make life go the way you want. What may work well for you in most situations may not work in others. There are no formulas, recipes, or step-by-step plans that guarantee success.

You may even think that if you don't get what you want, then you have failed in some way. But just because you don't get what you worked towards doesn't mean you are a failure. Is there only one possible way to be successful? Is there only one possible path to take? Who decided this? Often the things we don't plan for offer the greatest opportunities. Besides, who determines what it means to be 'successful'?

In fact, sometimes NOT getting what you want may be the best thing that can happen.

Clare desperately wanted a certain job and was devastated when she didn't get it. She kept looking and a short time later an even better job opened up. She applied, interviewed, and was hired. Now, if she had gotten the first job she wouldn't have still been looking and wouldn't have applied for the second job. Looking back, Clare realized that not getting the first job was the best thing that could have happened.

As inventor Alexander Graham Bell (1847–1922) said, "When one door closes, another door opens; but we so often look so long and so regretfully upon the closed door, that we do not see the ones which open for us."

Before his current position, Alfredo had two long-term jobs and they both progressed the same way. In the beginning he was the 'golden boy'. Then over a period of 10 to 12 years, management changed and the company politics became increasingly negative. He would find his efforts and performance questioned, and reassignment lurked in the future. But Alfredo kept a positive and forward-looking attitude. He focused on actions he could take, one of which was to look for a position elsewhere. The funny thing is, he always landed a better job at a bigger company. Now he is in his third position and it is the best of all. Thinking back over his career, he is thankful for the times when things were difficult. These difficult times pushed him to broaden his horizons and move on to bigger and better opportunities.

So to what does he attribute surviving this adversity and coming out on top? His positive attitude.

Things don't always progress the way you want. But if you keep your chin up and keep moving forward, you can make the best out of whatever life offers. Alfredo turned obstacles into opportunities. When life gave him lemons, he made lemonade.

How do you view your obstacles?

An old Buddhist story highlights this as well:

One day a poor farmer's only horse ran away. His neighbors said, "How will you plow your fields? This is bad." But the farmer said, "What's good, what's bad, who knows?"

The next day the horse returned, bringing other horses with it. His neighbors said, "Now you have many horses. This is good." But the farmer said, "What's good, what's bad, who knows?"

The next day when the farmer's only son tried to ride one of the new horses he was thrown off and broke his leg. The farmer's neighbors said, "Now your son cannot help you in the fields. That is very bad!"

To which the farmer replied, "What's good, what's bad, who knows?"

The following day an army came through the area and took all the strong young men to fight in a war. But they did not take the farmer's son because of his broken leg. The neighbors said, "Your son escaped going to war! That is very good!"

To which the farmer replied, "What's good, what's bad, who knows?"

You don't always know what will work out best for you. So plan and work hard, and then make the best out of what comes your way.

As you can see, there is no magic formula that guarantees success. Besides, how do you know that any one particular path is the best and only path you can follow to find your success? Remember, "What's good, what's bad, who knows?"

Musty thoughts: "I absolutely know certain things have to happen." "I've done everything right; I must get what I want." "I must get what I want to be successful."

Everybody hits a rough spot in the road of life now and then.

If you are going through a tough time, keep your chin up and keep moving. If you do, things will get better. But if you sink down and wallow in muddy, down thoughts, the rough times will last longer. When things are going badly, change gears and do something different, like volunteer. You can't help others without helping yourself too, and it's amazing how much smaller your problems can seem when you help someone else!

Remember, no matter what difficulties you encounter, other people have faced similar problems and survived. But there are also those who have faced similar problems and crashed. Which group will you be in?

Musty thoughts: "This shouldn't be happening to me." "I don't deserve this."

Problems don't magically disappear or solve themselves; you have to take action to help solve them.

When faced with certain problems, you may want to act like an ostrich and hide your head in a hole. But what does that solve? When you pull your head up, the problem is still there, and often it's even bigger because you haven't done anything to solve it. No matter how difficult the problem, the best way to get past it is to start working towards a solution today. Start with little steps.

Musty thoughts: "The solutions to my problems shouldn't be so hard or shouldn't take so long." "I must know the solution to this problem."

Getting ahead takes work.

You may dream or fantasize about how things might miraculously turn out. But miracles are rare. VERY rare. Most of the time good things don't happen just because you want them to happen. Good things happen because you take the steps necessary to make them happen. Getting ahead takes work, time, and energy. So if you aren't willing to put in the effort, don't waste your time dreaming of the rewards.

Musty thoughts: "I shouldn't have to work so hard." "This should be easier."

You are important, and so is everyone else.

There is no one in the whole world just like you. You are a unique blend of talents and experiences. So honor yourself and make something of those talents and experiences. But remember—EVERYONE is unique. So whether you are a great athlete, student, or musician, whether you win a contest, get elected, or are voted the 'most likely' to do something, you are not superior to or more important than anyone else. To see oneself as 'better than' others does not reflect confidence; it reflects arrogance. This is always welcome news to the many of us who didn't do any of the above. But each of us can remember a time when we felt superior to someone. We may have viewed them as weird or unimportant. But who are we to judge anyway? You have to see yourself as above someone in order to judge him or her. So this message applies to all of us. Respect all, no matter what.

> Before you criticize someone, you should walk a mile in their shoes. That way when you criticize them, you are a mile away from them and you have their shoes.
>
> Jack Handey, American Comic Writer and Comedian (1949–)

Musty thoughts: "I must be better than others." "I must be seen as better than others."

You are not a mind reader.

You don't know what is going on in someone else's mind. You may watch someone and try to interpret their thoughts, their mood, their wishes. But get real; you have no idea what is going on in someone else's head. Sometimes you guess that someone is upset with you or doesn't like you. But it's often just a guess. Their actions and mood may have nothing to do with you. So don't waste days, hours, or even minutes of your time worrying about what is going on in someone else's mind. Ask them, and then go with the answer they give. Work on and question your own thoughts instead of worrying about theirs.

Musty thoughts: *"I must know what they are thinking."*

You don't control how others view you.

You see yourself as shy; someone else thinks you are stuck up. You try to help; someone else thinks you are trying to take over. You think you are just being normal; someone else asks why you are in a bad mood.

You don't control how another person views you. They see you through their own eyes with their own thoughts, from their own perspective. You could spend all your time worrying about another person's opinion. You could go out of your way to try to influence their thoughts. And if you don't agree with their interpretations you could act in a way to try to prove them wrong or even argue with them, pointing out inaccuracies in their view. Or you could just relax, realize their opinion is just their opinion and not fact, and spend your time just being yourself. It's your choice.

Musty thoughts: *"They must see me the way I want them to see me."*
"They must not get the wrong impression."

When it really comes right down to it, you don't know much at all.

While you are walking down the street, someone rushes by and cuts in front of you. You criticize him and think to yourself, "how rude." What you don't know is that he is late for work because he stopped to help an elderly gentleman pick up a dropped bag of groceries.

When the cashier seems distracted and then snaps at you, you think, "what a terrible employee." What you don't know is that she was up all night with a sick child.

The person you judged as a self-absorbed snob because he walked by without even saying, "Hi," didn't even see you. He was preoccupied thinking about his mother's cancer.

You don't know why people act as they do. You don't know what they are thinking or hoping. You don't know what happened to them in the past or what is going on in their lives right now. You don't see things from their perspective. You don't know their concerns and haven't felt their fears. You may watch them and make a judgment. You may think they are kind, or weird, or happy, or anxious. You may think you know what they should or shouldn't do, how they should or shouldn't act. But when it really comes down to it, you don't know much about them at all. So, be careful not to judge.

When you judge others, you are basically saying, "I am better than you. I am all-knowing and I have the authority to decide what is right and wrong." But you really aren't. You are simply another human being trying to understand and navigate life. Judging is an act of superiority. You don't know why people act like they do and why things happen like they do. You can make guesses, but that's all they are—guesses. Tomorrow you may learn something new that causes you to completely change your mind.

A girl bought a book and a bag of cookies while waiting for her plane. She sat down, started reading her book and eating the cookies, only to be surprised that the man sitting next to her was eating her cookies too. She would take a cookie and he would take a cookie. As this went on she became increasingly upset. She thought he was rude, inconsiderate, insensitive, a thief, and many other unflattering things. She didn't say or do anything because she didn't want to make a scene. Finally there was one cookie left. The man took it, broke it in two, smiled, and gave her half. She was more than ready to leave when her flight was called and was still fuming as she took her seat on

the plane. Then she reached into her bag to pull out her book, and her fingers came upon something else: a bag of cookies. All of a sudden she realized that she was the cookie thief. She had been eating his cookies and he had willingly shared with her.

How often do we ABSOLUTELY KNOW FOR A FACT that something is a certain way, only to later learn something new that totally changes our view?

When it comes to judging others—DON'T.

You don't know why they act like they do. Heck, sometimes you don't even know why you act like you do.

When it comes to life, the more we know, the more we realize we really don't know much at all.

Musty thoughts: "It must be the way I think it is." "I must know why...."

What are some other realities about you?

Realities About Others

People won't always do what you want them to do.

That's for sure. But you know, you don't always do things the way they want either. Isn't this just the way life is? We're different. Everyone is trying to figure out his or her own life. Other people are focused on their wants and needs, and we are focused on our own wants and needs. So they are thinking about their life and what they want, and you are thinking about your life and what you want, and you do things differently. It's just the way it is.

Musty thoughts: "They must do what I want." "They must be the way I want them to be."

There is no such thing as a 'perfect' friend.

There is no such thing as a friend who does everything the way you like, wants to do everything you want to do, or believes everything you believe. So don't sit around and wait for that perfect friend to appear. Accept and enjoy your friends as they are rather than be disappointed or critical because they aren't exactly how you want them to be. If you are waiting for the perfect friend to arrive, you will wait your whole life and lose out on many enjoyable opportunities.

Musty thoughts: "They must like what I like and always do as I wish." "They must never disappoint or disagree with me."

Not everyone is going to like you.

As much as you may try, not everyone will like you. Just accept it. You could be the nicest, kindest, sweetest—any 'est' you can think of—and there will still be people who won't like you for their own reasons. Don't worry about or focus on them. Instead focus on people who do like you. Or even better, focus on liking yourself, and then share these positive feelings with others.

Musty thoughts: *"They must like me." "Everybody must like me." "They must think highly of me."*

You can't MAKE someone like you.

If someone you like doesn't seem to like you, move on. Find someone who does. When you grovel, or try too hard to get someone to like you, you look needy and weak. People admire strength. Like a magnet, the stronger you are, the more people are drawn to you. And the weaker you are, the weaker your attraction.

And make sure people are attracted to YOU, not to something you can do for them or something you can give them. If that is the case, they are using you. If you do things to try to keep them as friends, you are allowing yourself to be used.

You can't even make someone in your family like or love you. So, if there is someone in your family who treats your poorly, be nice but don't focus on them. If you scurry around trying to do everything you can think of to get them to like (or love) you, you are wasting your time. They can sense your need for their approval, and this makes them feel more powerful. In turn, they may become more steadfast in their rejection of you. Besides, their behavior has nothing to do with you; it reflects them—their thoughts, their feelings, their attitude. Keep your head high and know that you are fine as you are. You don't NEED their love and approval to be okay.

If someone treats you poorly and you put up with it, WHY? When you accept poor behavior, you are saying that that is all you think you deserve. You may get mad at the other person and argue that you deserve better treatment, but if you continue to associate with someone who treats you poorly, your actions speak louder than your words.

Musty thoughts: "I must make them like me." "They must approve of me." "They must be nice to me."

People can't take or steal your friends (boyfriends, girlfriends, husbands, wives...).

First, you don't own your friends. They have free will. So if they choose to be with someone else, no matter what the reason, it's a choice they made. Even if you think they were tricked or pressured into choosing the other person, ultimately it was their choice. No one forced them. Let it go. Find someone who wants to be with you. If you get mad at the other person or even get mad at your friend, it reflects you. You might think, "How dare they do this to me!" What do you mean, how dare they? They chose something different than what you wanted. Haven't you ever chosen something different than what they wanted? Should you control them, or should they control you? No. Move on. Angry people aren't attractive. Positive people attract.

Musty thoughts: "They must not leave me." "They mustn't choose others." "I must be their best friend."

Other people are NOT mind readers either.

Don't expect others to know what you are thinking or feeling. They cannot read your mind. That is why you have a mouth. Tell them what you want or what you are thinking. Tell them several times if you need to. 'Dropping hints' may not work. The other person really has no idea what is going on in your head. They may hear a hint, but since it isn't expressed as a strong request, they may just hear it as a preference—a preference that is really no big deal. Remember, other people are mainly focused on what is going on in their heads and their lives. So they may totally miss your hint. In fact, some people are so absorbed in their own thoughts and so focused on their own agendas that you almost have to hit them over the head with your request before they truly listen to you.

Musty thoughts: *"They should know what I'm thinking." "They should listen to me." "They should know what I like and what I don't like."*

Other people may expect or even pressure you to be the way they want.

Some people offer suggestions on choices you have to make in your life. They try to help you succeed or take an easier path. But others may expect and even pressure you to be the way they want. They may sweet talk you, get mad, try to punish you, criticize, or just keep telling you how to run your life. And if they do this, whom are they thinking about...you and what's best for you, or themselves? They are ME-MEs. They are using Outside Pressure to try to control

> The way I see it, if you want the rainbow, you gotta put up with the rain.
>
> *Dolly Parton, Singer, Songwriter, and Actress (1946–)*

you. But remember, their Outside Pressure can't work without Inside Pressure created by your own thoughts. So stop worrying about pleasing them and focus on your own life and your own choices. Accept the fact that people like this exist, and alter your behavior accordingly. Stay true to yourself and don't let others manipulate you.

Even if they say they know what's best for you, how do they know this? This is your life. This is your opportunity to make your own mistakes and grow and learn. Besides, who knows you better...them or you? So recognize when someone is pushing you to be the way they want and disregarding your wishes or feelings. Don't focus on trying to change them so they accept you or your choices. Focus on yourself and your dreams. If someone doesn't like you the way you are, move on and find people who do, or at least don't get caught up in pressure from people who want to change you.

Musty thoughts: "They must like and approve of me." "I must make them happy."

People may even expect you to be able to know what they are thinking.

If people are upset with you, it's best if they say so. To expect you to read their minds and figure out why they are upset is unrealistic. You may choose to ask them why they are upset. Then if they wish to discuss it, great, but if they don't, wish them well and move on. Life is too short to play the "guess what I'm thinking" game or the "I'm upset but I won't tell you why" game. When people expect you to be a mind reader, it reflects them and the way they handle life. They are creating their own unhappiness. Don't join their party. Choose to associate with people who are honest, up front, and talk with you about issues. Don't make your life any harder than it already is.

Musty thoughts: "Other people should be reasonable."

For some people "It's just Never ENough"

No matter what you do for them, It's Never ENough.

No matter how hard you work, It's Never ENough.

No matter how well you do, It's Never ENough.

These are "It's NEN" People. It's Never ENough.

So another person acts like your effort or performance is never good enough. Maybe they even act like you are never good enough. Now stop and think, does that reflect you and your thinking, or does it reflect them and their thinking? People like this can be difficult to be around, and even more difficult to live with. The truth is, no matter how hard you try, it may never be enough for some people. So if your goal is to please them, will you ever reach your goal? And if you think you can be happy only when you do please them, will you ever be happy? As much as you would love to receive approval and acceptance from them, let this go. The only person you really need approval and acceptance from is yourself. And when you aim for that, you stop giving others power over your feelings. You choose: spend a lifetime struggling to gain acceptance from others, or live your life for yourself. It's your choice.

When you try to please others, you may get angry because they are the way they are and then blame them for your anger. But where is that anger coming from? It's coming from your own thoughts and feelings. Are others responsible for your thoughts and feelings? Do you want to give this power away?

With some people, if you make a mistake and you apologize, It's NEN.

Even if you try to correct your mistake and make things better, It's NEN.

Even if you grovel, It's NEN.

When you mess up, apologize and try to make amends, but don't grovel. Some people will accept your apology, some people will forgive you, and SOME WON'T. For some people, you can never say or do enough for them to let it go. They seem to want to hold on to their anger and try to punish you, make you feel guilty, worthless, no good, or any other bad feeling they can make you feel (Manipulative Tricks). Apologize, do what you can to try to make things better, and then move on. How they act reflects them, and you can't do anything about them.

> **Life is a succession of lessons which must be lived to be understood.**
>
> *Thomas Carlyle, Scottish Essayist and Historian (1795–1881)*

Musty thoughts: *"They mustn't be the way they are." "They must be satisfied with me." "They must listen to me." "They must love me." "They must forgive me."*

You can't make someone else happy.

No matter what you do, no matter how hard you try, some people will never be happy. That reflects how they think about life. That reflects them. You can try to help, but don't base your happiness on

their moods. Anytime you let someone else's actions or attitude determine your happiness, you have given away power. Take it back. You control your happiness by your own thoughts.

Musty thoughts: *"Look at all I did. They should be happy." "I must make them happy."*

You can't change other people.

You may have the best intentions in the world. You may want someone to be happy or develop healthier habits so their life goes more smoothly. Or you may want them to change so your life goes more smoothly. No matter what your reason, you can't change someone else. They have to want to change and be willing to work at changing. You can reinforce certain behaviors or try to reason with and influence them. You can even set parameters and apply certain consequences. You could also reduce your contact with them. When you change how

you interact with that person, they may not change, but you change. And when you change, your life changes.

Musty thoughts: *"They must change." "I should be able to make them change."*

There will be dysfunctional people in your life, and some of them may be related to you (heck, sometimes it may even be you).

For one, we can all be dysfunctional at times. What does being dysfunctional mean? It means being unable to function normally and can be due to things like exaggerated emotions, irrational thoughts, depression, unrealistic expectations, inconsistent behavior, etc. When dealing with dysfunctional people, again, you can try to help, but don't base your happiness on their behavior or happiness.

Musty thoughts: *"They must be rational."*

What are some other realities about other people?

Realities About Life

Life is not fair; it's just life.

How many times have you heard someone say, "I don't deserve this!" Who deserves anything bad happening to them? Bad things happen to good people. That's life. Besides, who do we think we are to demand that life be the way we want?

"This shouldn't be happening to me!" Why not? What makes you immune to troubles?

"Why me?" Why **not** you?

"It's not fair!" You may be right. But does complaining make it fair or fix the problem, or does it just make you miserable?

Life isn't fair. It never has been and never will be. It's just life.

Do what you can to make things better, and at the same time learn to accept and appreciate what you have. Instead of complaining, focus on the positives. Besides, what good would it do you to fight it? Does fighting life make it better? Does it make it more fair? Does it make you happier? Does it improve your life in any way?

If you continually focus on the unhappy things in your life, they will grow and consume you. So focus on the positives. Be appreciative and loving, and you will find that the positives grow instead.

Musty thoughts: "Life must be fair." "This shouldn't be happening to me."

You won't always get what you want.

Nobody gets everything they want. And if you think your happiness depends upon getting something, then you are waiting for something outside to happen for you to be happy. You are allowing your happiness to be controlled by something out there. So are you really in charge? Do you feel powerful?

The truth is, you have power over your feelings because your feelings are controlled by your thoughts and attitudes. You choose what stories

The Joneses   **You**

you tell and what thoughts you have. You can choose to tell positive stories or negative stories.

Getting things is fine. We all like to get. But it's equally important to realize you can be perfectly happy without getting things. Happiness doesn't come from things or even other people. It comes from within you.

Plus, don't worry about keeping up with the Joneses. There will always be Joneses who have more and Joneses who have less. That's just reality. Relax and appreciate what you have.

Musty thoughts: "I must have it because I want it." "Things must go my way."

Life can be hard.

Who promised it would be easy? Look at the news, especially news from around the world. And you think you've got it tough? Eighty percent of the people in the world would trade places with you in a heartbeat. Life is life; learn from it, but don't fight it. If you had a rough start and were treated poorly, that's unfortunate. But you can choose to move on. Help yourself out. Treat yourself as the special person you are. Your personality style or your past experiences may make it more difficult, but what is your alternative—feeling sorry for yourself? How does that help you? There's an old saying, "When the going gets tough, the tough get going." So get going.

Musty thoughts: "Life shouldn't be so hard." "Life must be easier."

Seldom is there is a 'right way' to do things.

You do things one way. Another person does things differently. Sometimes one person thinks that their way is the right—and only—way to do things: the right way to eat, the right way to put items together, the right way to drive, the right way to comb your hair, the right way to.... Major arguments have ensued between individuals trying to convince the other person that their way is the right way. But is there really a right way? There may be a better way. There may be a more efficient way. There may be an easier way. But seldom is there a RIGHT WAY. In many cases, doing things the right way really means doing things 'my way.'

Musty thoughts: "They must do it my way." "They must do it right."

There is no such thing as a 'Perfect Life'.

Sometimes people think that if they do everything a certain way, they can have a perfect life. They may have caught a glimpse of someone else's life and think this other person has that perfect life, or they may just believe a perfect life exists out there somewhere. They may try to control people and events, demanding that things be a certain way. They put a lot of pressure on themselves and others to try to create this perfect life. But, there is no such thing as a perfect life where everything goes the way you want. And all the fretting and attempts to control only create new problems. Relax. Stop fighting life. Work at making your life better, and enjoy the ride along the way.

> It's not getting knocked down that defines you. What defines you is whether you get back up.
> *Anonymous*

Musty thoughts: "They must do things a certain way." "It has to be done this way."

There are no guarantees in life.

You could practice more than anyone and still not win. You could take all the necessary precautions and still have an accident or get sick.

You could hope and pray and wish or worry and fret all you want, and things still might not go the way you want. And what happened to all that time you spent hoping and praying or worrying? There are no guarantees in life, so to expect and demand them is a giant waste of time and energy. Go sing and dance and find things to enjoy in life instead.

Musty thoughts: "I should have won. I'm better." "I can't be in an accident." "Look at all I do right; I shouldn't get sick."

You don't control life.

You don't control what happens to you. You don't control other people or events. You DO control how you think and react, so you choose your attitude and actions. This is how you choose your life. And when life throws you a curve, you choose again.

We often have an idea of how we want our life to be, and reality may not match this vision. There will be struggles, there will be ups and downs, and there will be problems.

But as the author Theodore Rubin (1923–) once said, "The problem is not that there are problems. The problem is expecting otherwise and thinking that having problems is a problem."

Everybody has problems; we just don't know about their problems because we don't know all the things that go on in other people's lives.

It's not our problems that are important. What is important is how we choose to handle our problems. If you choose to keep your chin up, move forward, and be optimistic, then the problem doesn't run your

life; you do. But if you let a problem get you down, if you exaggerate it or demand that life be the way you want, if you feel sorry for yourself, or get angry...in other words, if you FIGHT life, then the problem has taken over. You have put it center stage, and now it dominates your story. You have given it power over your life.

Musty thoughts: *"I don't deserve this problem." "I must not have problems."*

What are some other realities about life?

Although you don't control life, you do choose the way you experience it! So our last reality is...*You Choose Your Life.*

You choose how you think. You choose what station you tune into the most, positive or negative.

You choose what thoughts and feelings you hold onto and what thoughts and feelings you let go.

All this affects how you act or react.

Which then affects what happens.

And then the cycle keeps repeating.

You could choose to be appreciative, kind, optimistic, respectful, gentle, sharing, industrious, and loving. And that would reflect you and affect what happens next.

Or you could choose to be demanding, negative, pessimistic, rude, inconsiderate, pushy, critical, and hateful. And that would reflect you and affect what happens next.

Which of these two approaches would make your life easier?

You don't have to be a brain surgeon to know the answer.

Why do people do this to themselves? I'm sure they didn't arrive on Earth and say, "Well, I think I'll fight life and make myself miserable. That sounds like a lot of fun." No, they just developed unhealthy habits.

Habits in the way they think.

Habits in the way they feel.

Habits in the way they approach life.

If you have developed habits that cause you pain, lead you to give your power away, or make you feel helpless and hopeless…change your habits. You can do this! You have the power to change.

So, take a good look at your life, and if you don't like some of your choices, choose again. You always have other options.

Use your brain to create peace in your life—not turmoil.

SIX SENSIBLE RULES TO LIVE BY

1. Things won't always go my way.

2. I'm not perfect, but I'm still okay (I am a perfectly imperfect human being).

3. Sometimes people do things I don't like.

4. Life isn't fair; it's life.

5. I recognize that I don't really know much at all.

6. I choose my life.

And if you find yourself being irrational and fighting life, ask yourself,

"Why? Is this helping me?
Is what I'm doing making my life better, easier, or happier?"

And remember, the great thing about life is you can always choose again.

Most people are about as happy as they make up their minds to be.
Abraham Lincoln, 16th President of the United States of America (1809–1865)

The final forming of a person's character lies in their own hands.
Anne Frank, German Jewish Author (1929–1945)

You often suffer more from your anger and grief
than from those very things for which
you are angry and grieved. (altered)
Marcus Antonius, Roman General and Politician (83 B.C.–30 B.C.)

You can choose to be happy or sad,
and whichever you choose that is what you get.
No one is really responsible to make someone else happy,
no matter what most people have been taught and accept as true.
Sidney Madwed, Consultant and Author (1926–)

I am still determined to be cheerful and happy, in whatever
situation I may be; for I have also learned from experience
that the greater part of our happiness or misery depends
upon our dispositions, and not upon our circumstances.
Martha Washington, First Lady of the United States of America (1732–1802)

The foolish man seeks happiness in the distance,
the wise grows it under his feet.
James Oppenheim, Poet (1882–1932)

6

Dropping
Unpleasant Feelings

Learning to Understand Your Feelings

As a baby you felt things, but you didn't know any words, so they were just 'feelings.'

You might have felt 'aaaa' (happy) or 'ucky' (sad), or maybe even 'ohhhhh' (scared) or 'yee-ha' (excited). Although you didn't know what to call it, you felt it. Some of these emotional memories were stored in your Emotional Brain. So even now, some of these memories, these feelings, can just spring up and alter your whole mood, and you may not even know where the feelings came from.

Then you started developing language and you began to connect words with their meanings. You learned that these feelings were called 'happy' and 'sad' or 'scared' and 'excited.'

As you learned more words, you started using them to think about your life and talk to yourself; your thoughts reflected your emotions, and your emotions reflected your thoughts.

Hopefully you learned more about your feelings, and the words connected to them, so you could better understand and express your wants and worries. But what if nobody around you talked about feelings, if this activity was never modeled? Would your vocabulary or understanding progress much beyond some of the basics? Would you learn to recognize, understand, reassess, and even release some outdated or irrational beliefs and feelings? It would be like learning to identify vehicles as cars or trucks but not progressing much from there. How complete would your information and understanding of vehicles be?

Or what if you were even told to stop feeling or acting certain ways, "Stop acting like a baby." "There's nothing to be afraid of." "Grow up; boys don't cry." So now you learn to deny your feelings. You learn to put on a mask and hide them from view. But your feelings are there. They are a part of you. Denying them doesn't make them go away. How can you understand, evaluate, reassess, or release something you don't acknowledge exists?

Once upon a time most of us believed in Santa Claus, and some of us were even afraid of that fat man with a white beard. But we grew up. We learned to see him differently. As you grow older and learn more, you realize that things may not be as you believed them to be. The more we learn, the more we understand and learn to let go of old, outdated beliefs and feelings. But what if we stopped learning to do this? We would still be stuck with beliefs and perspectives left over from our younger years or even just left over from yesterday. We wouldn't have

the skills needed to understand, question, or reassess, and to release unwanted, unrealistic, and outdated feelings and thoughts.

So learn about your feelings. Pull them out from behind the

mask and look at them; try to understand them. Learn to work with them, and more important, learn to release those that don't benefit you. You don't need to be afraid of Santa Claus anymore.

Adjusting Your Feelings

How do you get rid of unpleasant or negative feelings?

If you express your anger, fears, or hurts, doesn't that get rid of these feelings? Well, if you express your happiness or love, does that get rid of those feelings?

You may express and release negative feelings, but if an emotion is ingrained in your emotional memory bank you might just keep slipping into that mood without really knowing why. And if you keep creating negative thoughts, you will continue to create more negative feelings.

Remember, your feelings are like an onion. You may express the outer layers, but until you get to the message in the layers below, these same thoughts and feelings just keep showing up again and again (like a weed that you pull but that keeps coming back because you never get to the root).

Dealing with feelings seems difficult and can feel uncomfortable or even scary, so people often avoid peeling away the outer layers to get to the layers underneath. Besides, peeling can cause tears.

Some people think that in order to deal with and release their feelings, they have to analyze them—figure out the "when's" and "why's" and "how come's" and truly dig into their feelings. They may talk

about them over and over and over again. This is a messy process. No wonder people don't want to do this. Often the more you dig, the bigger the mess. Plus, you may turn around only to find that you didn't really get rid of anything. You just moved things around.

Some people are afraid of what they might find underneath the outer layers, so they avoid dealing with their feelings at all. They may think there is really something wrong with them that they have to hide. They really aren't as nice as they seem, they make mistakes, have problems, aren't smart enough, good enough, have bad thoughts. So they hide behind a mask and pretend everything is fine, hiding their true feelings about themselves.

The truth is, people often deal only with their surface feelings. This is where they feel comfortable, even though the surface feelings may be uncomfortable.

So, if anger is on the surface they may express it over and over, but they don't get to the feelings beneath the anger. Or maybe they have hidden their hurt and anger underneath a couple of layers of 'nice and happy,' and their true feelings rarely pop through. But they are still there, just below the surface. It takes a lot of energy to hide feelings.

But if you don't peel them away, these negative feelings never go away. They stay with you and you just live on the surface. And that becomes the story of your life.

But this is not the REAL you.

The truth about you is that if you could release all your fears, doubts, worries, judgments, criticisms, and hurts, you would find that you are more wonderful than you could ever imagine. When you release all those negative feelings, you are peaceful, loving, compassionate, accepting, and free. Your confidence soars. Your talents shine through. The negative voices in your head quiet so you can hear your answers. And your thoughts and actions reflect this inner peace.

You see, you are also like the ocean. Winds and storms whip around the surface of the ocean. But no matter what happens on the surface, deep in the ocean it is quiet, peaceful, and calm. You are the same way.

If you live on the surface, as most of us do, you get whipped around by people and events in your life. But when you live deep in your core, there is a quiet knowing and a calm acceptance of yourself that allows you to be peaceful and confident.

So how do you peel away at unwanted negative feelings to get to the core without a lot of pain, suffering, and drama?

One way is to question your thinking (discussed in the last two chapters).

Another is to accept your feelings, allow them to be, and then **LET THEM GO.**

The key is to not resist or rebel against emotions or to try to get around them by devising all sorts of tricks, but to accept them directly, as they are.

Takahisa Kora, Japanese Psychiatrist, Professor, and Author (1899–)

Accepting and Allowing Feelings

Why would you want to accept and allow a negative feeling? Isn't this book about making positive choices? This doesn't seem like a positive choice.

Well, if you were just going to accept and allow your negative feelings and wallow around in them for a long time, this would not be a choice that would improve your life. But the thing is, you need to accept and allow your feelings BEFORE you can let them go. And letting them go is the most important part of this plan.

You see, the harder you push a feeling away, the more you try to close your eyes to it and reject it, the harder it clings to you. You never get rid of it.

But when you accept it, allowing it to be, then you relax enough to **LET IT GO.**

It's like a child clinging to you. If you try to push the child away, they tighten their hold. But if you welcome the child, hug them and tell them how much you appreciate their presence, they relax, release their grip, and you can let them go.

So hold your feeling out. Look at it from all angles. Welcome it as something that has helped you get through life to this point. Accept it so it can release its grip on you, and then LET IT GO.

You may have to do this many, many times before you can truly LET GO. The great thing is that each time you do, you release a few more of those negative feelings.

Letting Go

Think back. Have you ever really wanted something—I mean, you thought you couldn't live without it? And then, all of a sudden something happened; you made a total shift and you just didn't care about it anymore? What happened to those intense feelings? You just **LET THEM GO.**

Or have you ever been really upset about something, then all of a sudden had a moment of clarity and the drama and upset feeling just seemed to drop away? For a period of time you were just at peace about this issue. Now, two hours later you might be upset about it again, but for that short period of time you just LET IT GO.

This is what it feels like: peaceful, calm, at ease with life.

Well, instead of just waiting and hoping that this LETTING GO will magically happen, you can learn to do this and, with practice, make it happen more regularly.

+ + HERE IS SOMETHING TO TRY

Focus on an issue that you are upset about. Start with something small, not something that is major in your life. Now allow yourself to feel however you feel about it. Feel it thoroughly. List off all the different words you could use to describe your feelings about this issue. Now take one of these feelings and do the following:

Where in your body do you sense it? Your neck? Stomach? Fist? The muscles in your arms or legs?

What words would you use to describe this feeling?

Now, take some slow, deep breaths and relax (let your muscles go) a little more each time you exhale.

Next, ask yourself these three questions. (What, more questions? Yes, questioning yourself is the only way you find YOUR answers.)

1. "Could I let this feeling go?" (Or, "Could I allow this feeling to simply be here?" Or, "Could I welcome this feeling?") Don't try to answer the question; just ask it. It doesn't matter if you would answer 'yes' or 'no.' Just by asking, you have recognized that you have a choice.

2. "Would I?" (In other words, "Am I willing to let this feeling go?") Again, don't worry about the actual answer. But if you get a strong sense that 'NO' you aren't willing to let it go, ask yourself, "Would I rather have this feeling, or would I rather be free?"

3. "When?" ("When will I let this feeling go?")

(continues on next page)

(continued from previous page)

4. **Repeat** these three basic questions as many times as you need until you get a sense of letting at least a little bit of the feeling go.

(This exercise is taken from The Sedona Method® *[www.Sedona.com] used here with permission by Sedona Training Associates.)*

More Examples:

I feel angry. I am tired of being pushed around. I feel resentful, hurt, unloved. My fist tightens. My eyes and eyebrows squint. My heart sinks. I feel lonely.

So let's start with lonely.

1. **Could I let this feeling go?** No. I would love to, but I can't seem to let it go. Could I allow this feeling to be here? Well, it is here. So instead of fighting it, just accept it as being here.

2. **Would I let it go?** I sure would.

3. **When?**

4. **Repeat** questions 1–3, still focusing on 'lonely' until you sense a shift in the intensity.

Now move to another feeling and continue.

1. **Could I let this feeling go?** Sit with this for awhile.

2. **Would I?**

3. **When?**

4. **Repeat**

But wait, if something unpleasant happens and you just release your negative feelings connected to this event, does that mean you just accept anything that happens to you? Does that mean people can treat you however they want and you just take it, and then you go off and release your feelings? That sounds weak.

No, this is not it at all.

Here is what it looks like when you release your negative feelings:

◆ You are calmer and more at peace;

◆ You don't create, and then keep repeating, negative stories;

◆ You don't get bent out of shape by some of the insanity of life;

◆ You recognize what you can and can't control;

◆ You are better able to use your Thinking Brain to help solve your problem or choose a course of action that works best for you;

◆ You don't waste energy fighting battles that don't need to be fought;

◆ You drop your fears and worries about yourself and recognize your true value, no matter what others say or do;

◆ You have a clear vision of what you do and don't want, what you will and won't accept;

◆ You are better able to calmly express your desires and stand your ground when you need to.

This is about getting to your peaceful core, the place where you are true to yourself and aren't swayed or affected by the various energies of the world around you.

When you operate from this level, you know what you want and behave in ways that are true to you. Your thoughts are clear and calm and you rarely have to ask, "Why did I do that?"

This is an area of immense personal strength—strength INSIDE YOU!

Just recently I started thinking about a regretful choice I had made. I was upset with myself, thinking about the pain I had caused someone I love. I cried, wishing I could go back and change things. I was sad and angry with myself, and I felt sorry for both of us. Then all of a sudden I **STOPPED.**

What was I doing?

How could feeling and thinking like this help me?

How could it help the other person?

It wouldn't change the past. And it doesn't improve the present or the future.

Why do I sometimes choose to think these thoughts, wallowing in the pain and guilt, and beating myself over the head for my actions? What do I get from doing this?

The best thing I could do for me and anyone else in this world is to learn from my mistakes and then let them go and move forward. Drop the drama, the tears, the self-pitying thoughts, and do something productive instead.

1. Could I drop this feeling?
    Yes.

2. Would I?
    Yes

3. When?
    Right NOW.

And that's what I did. In an instant I released these thoughts and feelings, and I was at peace.

Thoughts vs. Feelings

So which is most important, to work with your thoughts or to work with your feelings?

BOTH!

In fact, it's helpful to go back and forth.

If you are thinking a negative thought, stop and focus on your feeling. Describe this feeling. Feel it and try to let part of it go. Next focus on your thoughts again. What thoughts are connected to this feeling? Feelings elicit thoughts and thoughts elicit feelings.

> The greatest discovery of my generation is that human beings, by changing the inner attitudes of their minds, can change the outer aspect of their lives.
>
> *William James, American Psychologist and Philosopher (1842–1910)*

So now work with both. Focus on a thought. Question this thought. Then focus on the connected feeling. Feel it and learn to let it go. Then question the thought connected to this feeling. Then…back and forth.

In fact, here is a suggestion.

When thinking a negative thought, stop and totally focus on your accompanying feeling. Thought: "This won't work." Accompanying feeling: Disappointment.

Now increase the intensity. Exaggerate this feeling.

New intensified feeling: Devastated!

Stay with this intense feeling for a moment. Now listen to your thoughts.

New thought: "My life is ruined."

Often, your new thought will be exaggerated, demanding, or musty. In fact, sometimes so exaggerated, demanding, or musty that you chuckle at its absurdity.

Next thought: "Ya, right. I'll get over it."

Another suggestion—and this one has to do with thinking.

When you have a negative thought, take that thought and play with the words.

For example, if you think, "What if she's mad at me."

Repeat the basic statement but add some different words. "What if she never speaks to me again. What if she sticks out her tongue and gives me the raspberries? What if she eats bullets for breakfast and then shoots them at me whenever she sees me? What if she shoots missiles? What if she gathers billions of worms and dumps them in my house? What if she...." Play with the words. Be absurd. This may help you relax your original thought. "Well, you know what? What if she's mad at me? Life will go on."

Unpleasant Memories—Dealing with Past Regrets

Some memories of past regrets keep showing up. You think about them for two minutes one day and five minutes another. And when you think about them you get that same old upset feelings. Wishing you could change what happened is a total waste of time. You can never change the past. Getting mad or feeling sorry for yourself over and over is a waste of time. What good does that do anyway? Questioning your thoughts can help because you can begin to release some of the irrational thoughts connected to this memory. But, one of the main reasons this memory keeps returning is that it has a strong EMOTIONAL BASE. That's why you keep remembering it. It has strong emotional ties. So the next time this memory appears, instead of just thinking about it, focus on your feeling; welcome it, exaggerate it, question it, and learn to LET IT GO!

> Happiness is not in our circumstance but in ourselves. It is not something we see, like a rainbow, or feel, like the heat of a fire. Happiness is something we are.
>
> John B. Sheerin, Author and Editor

Dropping Anger–Learning to Forgive

Someone was mean to you.

It wasn't fair. It wasn't right. They said cruel things. They physically hurt you. Maybe it happened once, twice, or maybe it has happened for much of your lifetime. You are hurt. You shouldn't have been treated like this. You are angry. Don't you have a right to feel that way?

Sure you do! You have a right to feel any way you want to feel. It's your life.

But think of it this way.

They hurt you once (or twice, or hundreds of times), but if you keep thinking angry thoughts about it over and over and over again, who is hurting you now?

If you create a sad, negative, victim story about what has happened to you, who is affected by this story?

Does such a story make your life better? Or does it keep you soaking in the pain of the past?

That's not to say you should ignore reality and create some flowery, wonderful, perfect life story. But how you tell your story affects you and your life right now.

Tim's stepfather never liked Tim. He yelled at Tim and hit him when he didn't move fast enough. He kicked Tim out of the house when Tim was 17, and Tim hasn't been back since.

Tim's story could go like this:

He ruined my life. What a jerk. He yelled at me for no reason and hit me whenever he was in a bad mood. And my mom just stood by. She kept saying, "But what can I do?" I hate them both. I really got shafted in the parent department.

And Tim could carry this story around with him for the rest of his life. Or his story could go like this:

It was rough. I wouldn't want any kid to have to go through that. He's such an angry person. I moved in with friends. It was hard in the beginning. But

I kept in touch with people who loved and cared about me. And I got a good job, and I'm going to make my future better than my past. I refuse to let his actions ruin my life.

One story focuses on the past and the other person—how mean and cruel he was. The other story focuses on what Tim did and is doing to get his life together. Both stories are true. But which one is more likely to lead Tim to a happy, successful life?

Work hard not to let negative events or negative people play a major role in your story. If you give them a leading role, then you allow them to hurt you again and again and again as you keep repeating your story. This can happen even if you're just repeating your story to yourself. You don't need an audience to keep reliving the pain and making it stronger.

The best way to remove negative people from your story is to forgive them.

"But," you say, "why should I forgive them? They don't deserve to be forgiven."

That may be true, but this is not about them; this is about you and what's best for you.

Forgiveness is not about closing your eyes to what happened. It's not about saying what the other person did was okay. It's about releasing the hold it has over you—letting it go so you can move on with your life.

Holding on to anger, resentment, and hurt only gives you tense muscles, a headache, and a sore jaw from clenching your teeth. Forgiveness gives you back the laughter and the lightness in your life.

Joan Lunden, Broadcast Journalist and Author (1950–)

Holding on to anger, resentment, and hurt only keeps you repeating the stories from the past. Forgiveness allows you to create new stories for the future.

If someone tells you, either through their words or actions, that you are no good, stupid, undesirable, embarrassing, or worthless, is that really about you? Or do their words and actions reflect them—their feelings, thoughts, attitudes, the way they treat others, and the way they handle life?

How someone treats you reflects them and the kind of story they have created about life.

When we are young, we often adopt the messages that are sent our way, especially if those messages come from important adults in our lives like our parents or teachers. We think, "They are older, they know more than we do, they must be right." And once we believe this message, we make it part of our story. We notice times when these assessments are true. We start picking apart our actions, criticizing ourselves. We think it, feel it, and notice times when we can say, "See, it is true. I am no good, stupid, undesirable, etc." We may even start acting in ways to prove it's true. Or we could just give up and think it's useless to try to prove it wrong.

But wait, just because someone said we are no good, stupid, undesirable, embarrassing, worthless—does that make it true? Aren't those assessments just a result of the thoughts in their head? Don't their thoughts reflect them and their story? Is their story **THE TRUTH,** or is it just **THEIR STORY?**

Forgive them and let them go. Don't worry about their story. Just work on your own.

> ## Forgiveness is almost a selfish act because of its immense benefits to the one who forgives.
> *Lawana Blackwell, Author (1965–)*

Once you forgive, you are free to live again.

> ## Resentment is like taking poison and waiting for the other person to die.
> *Malachy McCourt, Actor and Author (1931–)*

Once you forgive you can stop focusing on the other person and start thinking about you and where you want to go with your life. Do you really want to carry around the thought of this person anymore? Do you really want to let this person continue to play a leading role in your story?

> ## When you haven't forgiven those who've hurt you, you turn your back against your future. When you do forgive, you start walking forward.
> *Tyler Perry, Playwright, Director, Producer, and Actor, (1969–)*

Forgiveness is not just important when dealing with others, it is especially important when dealing with ourself. Often the hardest person to forgive is ourself. That's why when we lay in bed we don't think of the two hundred good things we did during the day, but instead focus on the one or two or three mistakes we made. If we were meant to be perfect, we would have been made perfect. We are human. And part of being human is making mistakes. Learn from your mistakes and let them go. Don't let them play a major part in your story for the future.

Remember: don't look back, look forward.

Worry, Worry, Worry

- ◆ I have a pain. Maybe it's cancer.

- ◆ They didn't call. What if they were in an accident? What if they died? What if they forgot me? What if...?

- ◆ What am I going to do if I don't get that job? I'll be ruined. I'll lose everything.

- ◆ What if there is a tornado, an earthquake, or a flood?

- ◆ What if my girlfriend stops loving me; then what will I do?

- ◆ What if our plane crashes, boat sinks, bridge collapses, or elevator malfunctions?

Sometimes people create whole lists of things to worry about: *I could injure myself; what if we have a fire; what if my car dies in the middle of nowhere...?*

Sometimes people latch onto one particular issue and fret over and over about the possibilities connected to this: *What if I get AIDS? I can't get AIDS—that would be terrible; my life would be ruined; I just couldn't go on.*

Some people have even developed such a pattern of worrying that it becomes their pervasive mood and may not even be connected to any one particular thought; it's just an overall sense of fear. It may have been learned at a young age.

And if you worry, stop and think: *What does worrying really do for me? Does it protect me in any way from unpleasant events happening? Does it improve my life? Does it help me feel good? Does it help me focus on actions I can take to improve my life?*

Shantideva, an eigth-century Indian Buddhist, scholar wrote, "If you can solve your problem, then what is the need of worrying? If you cannot solve it, then what is the use of worrying?"

Worry is often wrapped up in DEMANDS ("This mustn't happen") and CATASTROPHIC THINKING ("If this happens it will be awful, terrible, horrible, shameful, or unbearable").

But first of all, you don't control the universe. You don't get to choose everything that comes into your life. What you can choose is how you handle what comes into your life.

> I've known many troubles big and small, but most of them never happened at all.
>
> *Mark Twain, pseudonym of Samuel Langhorne Clemens, American Author, Humorist, and Social Observer (1835–1910)*

And second, when bad things happen it may be difficult—very difficult—but you can move on, you can survive, and even eventually thrive, if you choose to.

Corrie ten Boom (1892–1083), a Christian Holocaust survivor who helped many Jews escape the Nazis during World War II, once said, "Worry does not empty tomorrow of sorrow—it empties today of strength."

So question your thoughts; don't let them spin out of control.

Recognize how it feels when you worry, and take a deep breath and learn to LET IT GO.

Feeling Sorry for Ourselves

Sometimes it's hard not to feel sorry for ourselves. Heck, even others may feel sorry for us. But what good does it do to feel sorry? Does it make things better? Sometimes we get stuck in that self-pity hole. We wallow around in the mud and can't seem to climb out. We tell the same story over and over, and it doesn't get any better.

It may help to realize that others have it worse. But that doesn't usually eliminate the pain we feel. We just want things to be different. But they aren't. And wanting and wishing doesn't improve our lives.

These feelings can be very hard to drop. But what is the alternative?

Remember, don't try to just ignore or push these feelings away. Accept them, value them, and then let them go.

Work on your story. Instead of focusing on how 'terrible' things are, focus on what you can appreciate.

If you lost your job, you still have your talents and there are other jobs.

If you messed up somewhere, you do other things well.

If someone you loved died, aren't you lucky you knew them?

If someone you loved left, well, you still have your health.

Or if you struggle with your health, you still have your family.

Or if your family is toxic, you still have...well, you still have something you can appreciate, even if it is something small.

Learn to appreciate what you have, rather than long for life to be different. Change your story to focus on the positive.

Whatever you think about grows because you spend time thinking about it. So if you focus on your sorrow, it will grow. If you focus on what you appreciate, it will grow as well.

Even though you may want to move forward in your life, you may have one foot on the brakes. In order to be free, we must learn how to let go. Release the hurt. Release the fear. Refuse to entertain your old pain. The energy it takes to hang onto the past is holding you back from a new life. What is it you would let go of today?

Mary Manin Morrissey, Minister, Counselor, and Author (1949–)

FEELING DOWN—AND BEING STUCK THERE

Moods can rise and fall like a roller coaster. People just naturally go through up times and down times. For some people, the roll is gentle; their ups aren't real high, their downs aren't real low and, perhaps more important, their downs don't last very long. Some people have even learned how to keep their mood at a fairly even and positive level. But for other people, the swing in moods can go from very high to very low, and some people even get stuck on the very low.

Now, you may like wild roller coaster rides. But this is about your moods. And being out of control or stuck at the bottom is definitely not going to bring happiness. You can work to control your mood swings by using some of the ideas presented throughout this book, but sometimes your brain chemistry takes over and it's difficult to control

your moods. That's when you need to ask for help. If you were on a roller coaster and it was out of control or stuck, wouldn't you ask someone to come help repair the ride? The same is true in life. If you are losing control or feel stuck, ask for help. Asking for help is a sign of strength, not weakness. Wouldn't you want someone you love to ask for help if they needed it? There are people who can help you work your way out of any rut. In some cases you may even benefit from chemical intervention to counteract the negative chemicals being created by your brain. But whatever you do, **DON'T GIVE UP**.

When people lose control or are down, it's natural to feel hopeless, like there is no end in sight. But there are ways to help gain control over our emotions, and most depressions don't last forever. There are many stories of people who have gone through emotional and depressed times, asked for help, and come out on the other side happier and stronger than ever, going on to lead long, fulfilling lives. Don't give up on yourself! **GET HELP!**

Talk to friends, family, counselors, teachers, coaches, or ministers. Talk to anyone who you think can be a positive influence.

If you don't know who to talk to,
here are some numbers you can call:

1-800-273-8255 (1-800-273-TALK)
1-800-784-2433 (1-800-SUICIDE)

We don't receive wisdom; we must discover it for ourselves after
a journey that no one can take for us or spare us.

Marcel Proust, French Novelist (1871–1922)

Wherever you go in the midst of movement and activity,
carry your stillness within you. Then the chaotic movement around
you will never overshadow your access to the reservoir
of creativity, the field of pure potentiality.

Deepak Chopra, East-Indian-American M.D., Author, and Lecturer (1947–)

It is only when we silence the blaring sounds of our daily existence
that we can finally hear the whispers of truth that life reveals to us,
as it stands knocking on the doorsteps of our hearts.

K.T. Jong

A man travels the world over in search of what he needs
and returns home to find it.

George Moore, Irish Poet and Novelist (1852–1933)

Learn to get in touch with the silence within yourself,
and know that everything in this life has purpose.
There are no mistakes, no coincidences,
all events are blessings given to us to learn from.

*Elisabeth Kubler-Ross, American (Swiss-born)
Psychiatrist and Author (1926–2004)*

7

Making Your Best Decisions

How can you make the best possible decisions, big or little? Remember, big decisions are often preceded by many little decisions. So first focus on making good little decisions; when you do, you won't face as many overwhelming big decisions.

◆ You don't have to stress over how you are going to get out of a messy situation, because your little choices along the way helped you handle this situation before it got messy and out of hand.

◆ You don't have to decide what to do about the report that's due tomorrow, because you prepared and worked on it along the way.

◆ You don't get stuck in a room with someone with whom you don't feel safe, because you made choices all along that made sure you weren't stuck in that room with this person.

> Row with the
> oars you have.
>
> *adapted from an*
> *English Proverb*

SO HOW CAN YOU MAKE YOUR BEST POSSIBLE DECISIONS?

Here are some suggestions:

Keep Healthy

A healthy body supports a healthy chemistry and results in a healthy outlook.

Eat properly. Like gasoline for a car, food is the fuel used to keep your body running. Some foods help you feel energized, and some foods cause you to drag. Unhealthy eating habits can contribute to depression and other diseases. Your engine will run best if you use the best fuel. But unlike gasoline, food is also used in the ongoing rebuilding of the vehicle itself. Cell by cell, your body is always regenerating. To build the strongest and most efficient vehicle possible, eat a balanced diet with

lots of fresh fruits and vegetables, and avoid sweets and unhealthy fats.

Exercise. Dance. Play soccer, or tennis, or even Frisbee. Get your body moving. Exercise strengthens and stimulates vital organs such as your heart and lungs, and increases the amount of oxygen available to your brain. It also increases the production and release of chemicals that help create a sense of happiness and well-being. When you feel better, your thoughts are clearer. So if you feel down, go for a walk. When you are angry, run. The physical movement alone can help you emotionally.

Learn to Reduce Pressure (Chapter 2)

Quiet the voices of others pressuring you to do and act how they want. Quiet the chatter inside that pressures you to listen to those outside voices. Most of the people in your life will come and go, no matter how cool or important you think they are right now. But you will be with you your whole life. So consider what's best for you. And remember that if someone is pressuring you to do something, they aren't thinking of you, they are thinking of themselves. So whom do you need to be thinking of?

Question and Drop Negative, Irrational Thoughts (Chapter 4 & 5)

Learn to control the urges of your Survival and Emotional Brain and instead use your Thinking Brain to analyze and plan. Count to 10 before you act/react. Give yourself time to think. Catch your negative and irrational thoughts early, and stop them before they snowball on you. And if they start spiraling out of control, question them. Don't let them go unchecked. Remember, just because you THINK something doesn't mean it's true.

Drop Negative Feelings (Chapter 6)

Learn to accept and then release negative feelings. LET THEM GO. Learn to forgive yourself and others.

Adopt a Positive, Loving, and Appreciative Attitude (This chapter)

Develop positive life stories that resonate with acceptance, forgiveness, love, and appreciation. Positive thoughts and emotions increase your problem-solving abilities and cause your brain to release chemicals that increase your positive attitude. On the other hand, negative thoughts and emotions reduce your ability to think clearly and cause your brain to release chemicals that increase your negative attitude. It's another cycle. (Which cycle would you rather be part of?) When you focus on happiness, love, and appreciation, you operate at your optimum level.

Learn to Be Centered, Relaxed, Balanced, and Focused (This chapter)

As you find peace within yourself, you will be better able to consult with, and listen to, your inner knowledge, intuition, and sense of what is right for you. Learn to respect and honor your inner voice of wisdom.

Adopt a Positive, Loving, Appreciative Attitude

(The Immense Power of Happiness, Love, and Appreciation)

Happiness is not just a mood or an emotion; it's a way of living. Happy people are more optimistic, energetic, accepting, forgiving, appreciative, expressive, and loving. Happy people tend to be better problem solvers, are open to new ideas, are willing to risk doing things differently, and try new things. They are more fun to be with and work with. And there is a physical component here too. Positive thoughts cause your brain and heart to release chemicals that help you feel happy.

Sad, negative thoughts and emotions drag you down. Your thoughts aren't as clear. You see fewer options and are reluctant to do things or take chances. You are pessimistic, have less energy, and are more judgmental and distant. Sad, negative thoughts and emotions cause your brain and heart to release chemicals that keep you down, which makes it even harder to pull yourself up.

So to make your best decisions, work on your happiness level.

How do you do this?

◆ Work on your life stories. Write a positive version of your story—or even just a chapter of your story. Read it, quietly and aloud. Add to it. Share it.

◆ Each day do something to help someone else. This not only helps others, but it feels good. Every time you help someone else, you help yourself.

- Choose friends who think positively, and avoid those who are negative and complain (or if you are around negative people, learn to tune out their negativity).

- Get up every morning and tell yourself something good is going to happen today. More often than not, it will be an accurate statement, and the confidence you gain by just saying that and watching out for the good stuff can make a huge difference in your attitude.

- Find a song that makes you happy, and sing it. Pick a song that can become the theme song of your life. Pick one with a strong message and tone, then sing it loud.

- SMILE. This is one of the simplest things you can do. Smile as often and as much as you can. It's hard to be sad when you smile. When you first wake up, lie in bed and smile for a minute or two. Smile when you are eating breakfast, on the bus, as you drive to work, even when you answer the phone. If you don't feel it, fake it. After a minute or two of faking it, you will start to feel more positive.

- Remember, what you focus on grows. So if you focus on being happy, your happiness grows. If you focus on disappointment, your disappointment grows. If you focus on 'wanting' to be happier, your 'wanting' grows. So focus on appreciation, and your sense of love and appreciation will grow.

LEARN TO FEEL GRATEFUL

- List 10 things you can feel grateful for—10 things you appreciate in life. List 20. Keep going until your mood shifts.
- Focus on different parts of your life. What are 5 things you appreciate about your family, where you live, the weather, food, sleep, friends, yourself, anything. Feel your appreciation.
- Look around and think of several things you can appreciate about everything you see.

(continues on next page)

(continued from previous page)

◆ Start a Gratitude Journal to help you focus on the good in your life. Review your entries in this journal and add new ones each day.

Now take one thing for which you are grateful and focus on it. Relax, close your eyes, and let yourself experience how it feels to appreciate this item, person, or event. Feel it in your heart, then let this sense of appreciation flow through your body. Imagine your heart reaching out and embracing this item, person, or event. Hold on to that feeling for several minutes. Appreciation is filled with love, so imagine your heart getting bigger and bigger as it encompasses the love you have connected to this item, person, or event. This is probably the highest-level feeling you can feel.

Focusing on appreciation doesn't change the facts of your life; it changes you, both physically and emotionally.

And when you change, your life changes.

A friend recently went to the dentist to have new work done. Lying in the chair dredged up body memories of the old, slow drills and the pain and fear that went along with extensive dental work over the years. She felt tense and stressed. So she tried something different. Instead of fighting the tension and reminding herself to relax, she focused on FEELING appreciation. She thought of all the things she was grateful for at the dentist's office. She was grateful for the anesthetic to numb the pain. She was grateful for the new tools that made the work more efficient. She was grateful for the new techniques that made it go faster. She was grateful for the comfortable chair, the friendly and gentle dentist, and on and on. She spent the whole time not just thinking grateful thoughts but FEELING grateful. As a result, her body relaxed. By focusing on FEELING grateful and FEELING appreciation, she naturally became calm. She was amazed at the transformation. She had never had such a pleasant experience at the dentist's office.

FOCUS ON YOUR HEART
AND FEEL THE LOVE

It's not just thinking loving, grateful, and appreciative thoughts that seems to provide the most benefit; it's the act of FEELING love, gratitude, and appreciation. These feelings seem to emanate from the heart. And scientists have discovered that the heart plays a major role in our emotional well-being.

The heart has its own nervous system, and there is a two-way communication between the heart and the brain. Your emotions affect the rhythm of the heart, which is then communicated to the brain. The heart also secretes hormones that influence your brain. Based on this information, a non-profit organization called The Institute of HeartMath® (http://www.heartmath.com) developed exercises that specifically focus on the heart.

They suggest that while you relax, you focus on your heart and learn to activate feelings that radiate from your heart, like care and appreciation. Doing this reduces stress and creates inner peace, which improves both your emotional and physical well-being.

Thinking about love and gratitude is important. But it's even more important to FEEL grateful, appreciative, and loving. Feeling this way is probably the most important thing you can do to improve your life. It not only creates a positive perceptual shift, but it also creates a biophysical response that benefits all areas of your life, from your thought patterns to your stress level to your health.

And remember, what you focus on grows. So if you are focusing on thinking loving and appreciative thoughts, these thoughts grow. And if you focus on feeling loving and appreciative, those feeling grow.

Being Centered, Relaxed, Balanced, and Focused

To understand the importance of being centered, relaxed, balanced and focused in your life, think of the martial arts. When you watch people demonstrate martial arts, there is a calm gracefulness; each movement has a purpose and there is little wasted energy. They are open and aware, yet focused and centered. Basically, it is peaceful powerfulness.

Wouldn't it be wonderful if you could use those same words to describe your life? Centered, calm, graceful, purposeful, focused, open, aware, efficient, peaceful, and powerful.

If you could handle life in this way, things would just flow. You would become the most successful YOU possible.

This powerfulness is not about power over things or people; it is a sense of power within you—personal power, a sense of comfort and confidence about yourself and the direction you are headed. It is the opposite of being anxious, stressed, confused, afraid, or angry.

So how can you increase your sense of personal peace and power and feel centered and balanced?

Learning to live in love and appreciation helps to create a positive and more peaceful attitude.

> At the center of your being you have the answer; you know who you are and you know what you want.
>
> *Lao Tzu, Chinese Philosopher (6th Century B.C.)*

Questioning your thoughts and feelings, and releasing those that are unproductive and stressful, helps to find your center and balance.

You see, finding your center, your core, the true you, is not about building or adding something to what is already there; it's about clearing away negative, time-wasting, unproductive, energy-consuming emotions, thoughts, and activities so you can discover what's already there. It's about focusing on love and appreciation so you learn to honor and value everything and everyone, especially yourself.

Learn to RELAX

Learn to Let Go Physically

So many times we think we are relaxed, but if we do a body scan (mentally think through the different parts of the body) we find tension somewhere. So learn what it feels like to really be relaxed.

Relax Your Whole Body

Start by tensing up your whole body, every part of it. Squeeze as tight as you can for several seconds. Then let go and relax. Do this several times. The most important part of this is to feel what it feels like to 'let go.' In fact, when you let go, try to keep letting go more and more and more. Can you feel yourself dropping or sinking deeper and deeper into a relaxed state, or feel your limbs getting heavier and heavier? Even when you think you've let go there is usually even more to let go. Learn to recognize what this feels like.

Relax Different Parts of Your Body

Now work on different parts of your body, starting with your toes.

Tighten the muscles in your toes—then let go. Do this several times and remember to keep letting go.

Next repeat this tightening and letting go exercise as you move your way up your body to your foot, ankle, calf, etc. Learn what it feels like to let go and to keep letting go. See if you can isolate certain muscles as you tighten and release them. Work at really feeling your body from the inside out.

Our society moves so quickly that many people have lost touch with their bodies. People carry stress and don't even realize it. We pick up

more information than our brains can ever process, and our bodies'
responses just may be the signals we need to let us know that something is or isn't right. But we're too busy to even realize it.

So learn to focus on your body. At different times throughout the day
take a minute to do a body scan; thinking through your body, find any
tension, and release it. See if you can feel your heart beat. Relax. Breathe.

Learn to Breathe Properly

So, now that you are relaxed, do one more thing. Put
your hand on the top of your belly and feel what
happens when you breathe. You should feel your hand
moving up and down with each breath. This is how you
breathe when you are relaxed, like when you are falling
asleep. You breathe low towards your abdomen, not
high towards your shoulders. Often, when people take a
deep breath they take a big breath where their shoulders
rise. But the largest part of your lungs is low, towards
your abdomen. So when you want to take a nice, slow, relaxing breath,
this is the direction to take it. Imagine filling your stomach with air as
you inhale. Once you start breathing this way you will realize how
much more relaxing this is than the high, shoulder breathing.

Why is breathing so important? Well, try to stop breathing for a
while and see what happens. Seriously, breathing brings oxygen into
your lungs, and oxygen supplies life to all parts of the body—especially
your brain. Deep breathing also helps you slow down,
focus on the now, and become centered. When your
emotions get a little out of control, when you're
scared, worried, angry, or upset, one of the best things
you can do is stop and take a few deep breaths. Slowly
take a breath in, towards your abdomen, towards your
center, then slowly let it out and repeat it 10 times or
more. You will be able to feel some of the tension and
negativity slip away. While you are doing this you can

do a body scan to see where you notice tension, and let it go. Doing this helps your emotions settle down. Now instead of them running you, you are in control.

Honor Life by Focusing on the NOW

We are often going so fast that we fail to appreciate the wonders of life. Take time each day to stop and focus on what is going on around you right NOW. Smell the air. Look at the clouds. See that flower pushing its way through a crack in the cement. Just look around and try to notice all the wonderful things in the space that surrounds you. Look at the plants and animals and honor their daily struggles and needs. As you look at man-made items, think about how these items came to be. Think about and honor all the different people who were involved in the process. Learn to appreciate all aspects of life. Breathe deeply, and honor the air that sustains you. You can do this in short snippets of time as you walk from the refrigerator to the table, when you walk outside, while you are waiting your turn somewhere. It helps you slow down a little and tune into the NOW rather than just having your mind wander all over the place. Plus, giving thanks for all the different parts of life adds to your sense of wonder and appreciation.

> The more tranquil a man becomes, the greater is his success, his influence, his power for good. Calmness of mind is one of the beautiful jewels of wisdom.
>
> *James Allen, (British-born) American Essayist (1864–1912)*

Meditate

So what's so great about meditating?

Meditation is more than just sitting quietly. Through meditation you learn to drop the stories and thoughts that usually run out of control, leading you in the wrong direction, and learn to listen to your inner voice, which is often lost in all the noise. Meditation helps you develop a peaceful, accepting, centered, and open state of mind.

If you've ever zoned out while staring into a candle flame or the flickering of a fire, or a sunset, you know that when you came back to attention you felt relaxed and calm. That's similar to what meditation feels like.

The benefits of meditating on a regular basis are immense.

First, it has been proved that continued meditation practice reduces stress. It allows you to slow down and become more centered, peaceful, and calm. Your thoughts become clearer, less cluttered. When you feel peaceful you have a more positive view of life. In turn, your  actions will reflect this attitude and have a positive impact on what happens to you. It's the Choicycle.

The effects of meditating spiral outward, affecting every part of your life. Meditating benefits your body, your actions, your choices, and your relationship with yourself and with others.

This doesn't happen overnight. At the same time, it also doesn't require you to become a hermit or a monk. You can reap great benefits from meditating just 10 to 15 minutes a day. Just a short amount of time each day will affect your whole life.

Second, as you become more adept at meditating, you learn to quiet your thoughts for longer periods of time. You learn to stop that mental chatter, so you can hear your answers from deep inside. This is nothing weird. We all have our own answers deep inside. It may be intelligence beyond the brain, or maybe it is information from our brain that we can't hear because of all the mental noise. Wherever it comes from, we just have to stop our minds long enough to hear it. Call it our subconscious, intuition, or an inner guide—it doesn't matter what you call it. It's there in all of us. It's our inner voice of wisdom.

It's the REAL YOU

It is the YOU that's underneath all those fears about not being okay and the worries that your life won't go the way you want.

It's the YOU that believes in YOU and is realistic and respectful of YOU.
It's the powerful YOU.
Meditation helps you find this YOU.

Have you ever had a problem, then all of a sudden you had a breakthrough? All of a sudden you saw it from a new perspective. Some people call it an 'Ah ha' moment, when for some reason everything became clear and you 'got' it. When you are able to quiet your mind, even for short periods of time, you start seeing and understanding life from a different perspective. As you meditate, you open yourself to more and more of these insights.

SO HOW DO YOU MEDITATE?

First off, there is no right or wrong way to mediate. You don't need to sit cross-legged with your palms up. You don't need to chant 'Om.' You don't need to sit for long periods of time. In fact, you might try to start meditating for just 5 or 10 minutes a day. It would be better to meditate for shorter times and do it consistently than to aim for longer times and do it less often.

Step-by-Step Guide Remember, there is no RIGHT or WRONG way.

You may want to do some stretching prior to starting. You also may want to set a timer so you don't focus on worrying about time.

1. Find a quiet place, free of distractions.
2. Get comfortable. Sit on a pillow or sit in a chair. It doesn't matter, just as long as you are comfortable.

(continues on next page)

(continued from previous page)

3. Close your eyes and start relaxing, letting go.

4. Take a deep, slow inhale, and then just as slowly release the breath. Breathe deeply into the lower part of your lungs.

5. While you are breathing you can repeat the words, 'In' (as you take a slow breath in) and 'Out '(as you release your breath). You may even want to count your breaths to help you stay focused on breathing.

6. Now as you slowly breathe, relax your body starting with your toes and working your way up.

7. Once your whole body is relaxed, go back to focusing on your breathing.

8. Feel the air coming in and going out.

Additional questions, notes, and suggestions

◆   Focusing on your breathing helps you clear your mind and quiet the mental chatter. So as you notice your mind wandering off into random thoughts, bring your focus back to your breathing; slowly inhale, exhale, and relax.

◆   How do you stop your mind from thinking and wandering? Now that is a really good question that people have been trying to figure out for centuries. (So if you get any good ideas, let everyone know.) Try focusing on your breathing again. Count breaths. Try focusing on relaxing different parts of your body. Try focusing on a word, such as 'peace' or 'love' or 'acceptance.' Focus on the feelings connected to that word. But most of all don't get upset if your mind keeps wandering off thinking of things. Just notice it, smile, and go back to focusing on your breathing. The more you do this, the easier it becomes.

◆   If you have trouble relaxing because you have a lot of pent-up emotion, you might ask yourself questions designed to help you LET GO. *(Discussed in Chapter 6)*

    1. Could I let this go?

    2. Would I?

    3. When?

(from The Sedona Method®—*used with permission of Sedona Training Associates)*

So to make your best decisions, listen to yourself—your core, the true you that is often covered by your fears and negative thoughts. Learn to be relaxed and centered. And remember, FEELING grateful and appreciative is probably the single most important thing you can do to improve your life. So focus on your heart and let your love and appreciation expand. When you do all this you will be better able to tune into that inner voice of wisdom that truly knows what's best for you.

> The happiest people don't have the best of everything. They just make the best of everything they have.
>
> *Anonymous*

It is through science that we prove,
but through intuition that we discover.

Jules Henri Poincare, French Mathematician (1854–1912)

Good instincts usually tell you what to do long before
your head has figured it out.

Michael Burke, Business and Sports Executive (1918–)

The intellect has little to do on the road to discovery.
There comes a leap in consciousness, call it intuition or what you will,
and the solution comes to you and you don't know how or why.

Albert Einstein, American (German-born) Physicist (1879–1955)

You are a living magnet. What you attract into your life
is in harmony with your dominant thoughts.

Brian Tracy, Business and Personal Management Author and Speaker (1944–)

Silence is the great teacher, and to learn its lessons you must
pay attention to it. There is no substitute for the
creative inspiration, knowledge, and stability that come from
knowing how to contact your core of inner silence.

Deepak Chopra, East-Indian-American M.D., Author, and Lecturer (1947–)

Most of us are in touch with our intuition whether we know it or not,
but we're usually in the habit of doubting or contradicting
it so automatically that we don't even know it has spoken.

Shakti Gawain, Personal Growth Author and Speaker (1948–)

8

Intuition–
Your Inner Compass

What Is Intuition?

Intuition is that higher knowing—knowing something without really knowing how you know it. People call it a 'sixth sense,' 'inner wisdom,' 'gut feeling,' or a 'hunch.' It's an insight into your life where you sense what is going to happen, a direction to head, an action to take, or what is right or wrong. It seems just to come to you. Your intuition can help with many choices. It is your Inner Compass.

Now, with that said, part of intuition is explainable.

Trust your hunches. They're usually based on facts filed away just below the conscious level.

Dr. Joyce Brothers, Psychologist and Television Personality (1949–)

141

The Explainable, Part 1–Your Awesome Brain

Your brain processes more information than you can ever attend to. You hear, see, sense, and smell things that you aren't even aware you heard, saw, sensed, or smelled. While you listen to your friends talk, you pick up information from your environment: sounds, movements, everything and everyone you see. You notice people's body language, such as eye and hand movements, shoulder placement, voice inflections, how people orient themselves in relation to others, and much more.

In some ways your mind is like a video camera. While you focus on your friends and the conversation, the camera also records volumes of other information. You are not consciously aware of this information because you weren't focused on it. But it is recorded in your subconscious, and without even knowing it, you then pull from it for ideas and opinions.

Most of the information you record in your subconscious is unimportant. But sometimes this information starts to germinate and grow into an idea. Or it could cause you to form an impression or an opinion of someone or some event. And in some cases it can even set off an alarm that something doesn't seem right. But since this information is subconscious, you don't know where these ideas, opinions, and impressions come from. They just seem to appear as a gut feeling, a hunch, or an intuition.

Gavin DeBecker, a national expert on predicting violent behavior, uses an example of this in his book *The Gift of Fear*. DeBecker tells the story of a gentleman who, upon entering a convenience store, suddenly felt he should leave, and so he did. Several minutes later a police officer walked into the same store and was shot by a person attempt-ing to rob the store. The first gentleman had a sense that something wasn't right but couldn't identify it other than saying it was just a 'gut feeling.' Only later as he dissected the event did he realize he had picked up multiple clues to warn him: the quick glance by the clerk at the cash register; the man wearing the coat in the middle of the summer; the way the clerk looked at the man in the coat. All of these were clues, signals picked up by the gentleman entering the store. At the time he didn't recognize their meaning; he just sensed something wasn't right.

> What lies behind us and what lies before us are tiny matters compared to what lies within us.
>
> *Ralph Waldo Emerson,*
> *Essayist and Poet*
> *(1803–1882)*

DeBecker suggests that our instant sense of apprehension and fear is a gift telling us that we need to be on the alert. He isn't talking about the worries and fears created by the stories we make up in our head, but about the instantaneous thought, sense, or gut feeling that just flashes, telling us to 'beware.' Often these gut feelings are based upon clues that we noticed at a subconscious level. There are many stories of people who honored this message from within and were later grateful they had, as well as stories of people who discounted this message and talked themselves into trusting or believing that there was nothing wrong, only to later wish that they had listened to that little voice inside.

The Explainable, Part 2–Your Wandering Mind

Another part of intuition that is understandable is that your mind works 24/7. It's always on the move. You can be in the middle of some-thing, and BAM! You come up with an answer to a problem totally unrelated to what you were doing at that moment. Where did that answer come from? Your mind must have wandered over to some sub-conscious area and made a connection.

One of the reasons it is so important to have a calm mind and drop negative thoughts and feelings is that it frees up your mind to wander

and find more of your answers. Wandering is not the same as going back over the same problems again and again. Wandering is free and relaxed—where you meander into new territories and possibly even access subconscious ideas and thoughts.

Even when we sleep, our mind stays active. But in sleep we don't direct our attention to any one area; our mind just seems to float around on its own and come at our problems from a very different angle. Plus, it can access all the information that we know but didn't realize we knew. That's why people often wake up with an insight or an answer to their problem. And the same thing can happen when we daydream. As we let our mind wander, it can access information that is stored who knows where.

Here again is another reason to release negative thoughts and feelings. If you spend much of your day focused on negative, worrisome stories, then at night, or when you daydream, your mind will gravitate towards these, and most likely you will have negative, worrisome dreams. This doesn't allow your mind time to float to find new answers, ideas, or insights.

The Explainable, Part 3–Connecting with Our True Core

On the surface, we show our social mask and our exterior feelings. But at some level we know what is right for us and what we truly do and do not want to do. We may say we like the pineapple strudel because we want to please or impress someone, when we know we really don't like pineapple. We may say, and even think, something isn't bothering us when at a subconscious level we are stressed over it.

Our intuition, gut feelings, and hunches often connect with the real us buried beneath layers of confusion, social pressure, personal worries, bravado actions, and false assertions that we really don't care. It slices through these layers of denial and avoidance and goes to the core of what we truly feel and believe. Our intuition is a message from the real us. And that's where our truths lie.

So sometimes intuition, gut feelings, or hunches originate from the subconscious information obtained about our world. Sometimes it comes from our mind that is working 24/7, and as a result covers territory we don't consciously think about. And sometimes intuition comes from our own special knowledge about ourselves at the core level.

But then there is a whole other part of intuition that is unexplainable. At least it's unexplainable as in not being logical or even able to be tested by today's science.

The Unexplainable

When Jane was traveling through South America she started having troublesome dreams about her sister. This had never happened before, so Jane was concerned. When she was finally able to get to a phone and call home, she learned that her sister had been in an accident. Her sister survived but was still hospitalized.

How did Jane know something was wrong with her sister? She didn't pick this up from clues in her environment stored at a subconscious level. She didn't find it with her wandering mind. And she didn't get this information from her core being. So how do you explain it?

I knew an intuitive lady that for years prior to September 11th, 2001, knew something was going to go terribly wrong on a transcontinental flight. People would consult her prior to any cross-country trip to see if she sensed their flight was safe. Over time she became even more specific about the flight. She said it would originate on the East Coast. Then 9/11 happened. How did she know this?

There are countless stories of people who all of a sudden knew they needed to take a different path, a different flight, stop, or leave, and lived to value this message. All of a sudden they got an impulse that said, "Don't go there." And they heeded that impulse. They listened to their inner voice.

Or, even closer to home, and more common, has the phone ever rung and you knew who it was before you even answered? Or you knew the exact words someone would use before they even spoke? How do we know these things?

Most people have experienced déjà vu where all-of-a-sudden everything seems familiar, like they have been there before. And where does this come from?

Some day, as science advances, we may be able to explain these intuitions scientifically. But for right now they just seem supernatural.

But remember, once upon a time, not too long ago, we didn't know about x-rays and infrared, and although we can't see them, we now know they exist. What else exists out there that we can't see or we don't even know about yet? We look back at people who lived a hundred years ago and think how naive they were, and how little they knew. Well, a hundred years from now, people will look back at us and think the same thing.

But, then again, maybe there is no scientific explanation for some of the things people sense. They just sense them.

So no matter whether your intuition is explainable or unexplainable, you want to listen to this information. It is a higher knowing, where you consult your subconscious, your core, or who-knows-what else. Your intuition knows what is best for you. It provides an insight into your life where you sense what is going to happen, a direction to head, an action to take, places or people to avoid, or what is right or wrong. And it seems to just come to you.

Learn to listen to and honor these instances of 'knowing.' They provide guidance in your life.

RECOGNIZING AND DEVELOPING YOUR INTUITION

Intuition comes in many ways. It can come as a:

◆ still, quiet, inner voice;

◆ dream;

◆ sense that something is right or wrong;

◆ physical sensation of feeling heavy, or a tightness in your chest, or 'the chills' or a 'creepy' feeling;

◆ physical sensation of lightness or a surge of energy;

◆ flash of understanding and knowing;

◆ vision of a direction to take;

◆ coincidence—you hear (or see) something, and then it seems just by chance you hear (or see) it again somewhere else.

Unless it's a major jolt, like fear, the information will often be quiet and easily overlooked. The message will not be blatant and to the point. It will not hit you over the head with a sign that says, "**DO THIS.**" It will be just a sense, a feeling of what to do.

So what can you do to increase the chance that you pick up these intuitive messages?

First, learn to recognize and honor these valuable insights.

When was a time you just knew what you should do?

Or an answer just came to you?

Or you sensed something wasn't right?

Think of a time that you had a feeling about something or someone and you ignored it or argued against it, only to say later, "I knew I should have...." Or, "I shouldn't have...." Or, "I sensed they were...."

That was your intuition speaking to you, but you totally blew it off and went ahead and listened to your mind.

Often you don't even realize you 'blew it off' until later when you remember you had that sense, that 'knowing' about a person or event.

Pay attention to these times. The more you pay attention, the more you will notice them happening.

Even after a rain, a desert still looks dull and muted. There doesn't seem to be much color. But if you look closely, you will notice little bits of color on tiny flowers here and there. You could walk right by and not even notice them because they are so small and subtle. Once you start noticing them, however, you begin to see more and more color. But you need to look quickly; they won't last long.

> Intuition does not always appear as the ingenious breakthrough or something grandiose. Intuitive thoughts, feelings, and solutions often manifest themselves as good old common sense. Common sense is efficient.
>
> From Chaos to Coherence *by Doc Lew Childre and Bruce Cryer (2000).*

Intuition works the same way. It is often subtle and easy to overlook. It comes quickly and then it's gone.

As you start to pay attention, you might be surprised how often these instances of intuition happen. So note them, maybe even keep a journal, and honor them.

Remember, they are small and quiet.

Second, do things to increase your chances of noticing this information. In other words, know what you're looking for, walk slower, maybe even water and fertilize so more color shows up.

WHAT YOU CAN DO

Meditate

By meditating, you open yourself to receive more of these subtle messages.

Ask for answers

Right before you go to sleep, relax and ask yourself for the answer to your question. You might even write your question on a sheet of paper. Then when you wake up, think about this issue again and see if you received any messages in a dream, or if you have any new insights, ideas, or gut feelings.

Before you meditate, ask yourself questions about things in your life, decisions you need to make, and problems you have. Then as you meditate, listen for the answers. If your mind starts going off, telling you what to do and thinking about all the things related to the issue, stop it. You already know those things; you've thought them a hundred times before. You are looking for new information, or at least quiet information that you may have overlooked. Go back to focusing on your breathing, quiet your mind, and listen again.

If you get answers or thoughts or impressions, notice if your mind starts arguing against this information.

"Yeah, right. I can't do that."

"But they look so nice. I should trust them."

"What if they get mad and don't want to be around me?"

"It won't be that bad."

"Look what she's done for me. I can't say 'No.'"

No matter what your mind says, no matter how many arguments it can present, remember that your intuition has your best interests at heart. Your intuition knows the truth.

(continues on next page)

(continued from previous page)

Write

When you are relaxed or just after you have meditated, write. Write whatever comes to mind, just let it flow. Even if you write, *"I don't know what to say,"* over and over, just write. Or you could think of a problem and then just write whatever comes to mind. Pretty soon some of your intuitive thoughts will come through.

Doodle

Think of your problem, then put it aside and just doodle. Get lost in your doodling. Don't push for an answer. Just doodle and see what comes. If you have a choice between two options, write one option on the left side of the paper and the other option on the right side. Then doodle away, and pay attention to which option you seem to be pulled towards.

Remember, intuition is often just a quiet sense about what feels right. As soon as you find yourself arguing, *"But it won't work."* Or, *"It will be all right. I'll just do it this once."* Or, *"But I really, really want to."* **STOP.** All that is your brain talking. What is your intuition saying?

It Could Be

Do you remember having those 'instant feel good about yourself down to your bones' moments? You may have done something you were proud of or had a sudden good feeling about yourself for no particular reason. Then something or someone came along and either knocked you down or brought you out of the clouds. Or maybe even you were the one to snap yourself out of that feel-good moment. You'd say, *"You're not that good."* Or, *"Yeah, right. Get real."* Or, *"Who do you think you are anyway?"* Or, *"You can't do that."*

Well, maybe that instant, 'knowing' in your core that you were awesome, was really your intuition kicking in. Then life happened and you let it pull you back.

Remember those times when you've thought, *"Why did I do that? I knew I shouldn't have...."*? Well there are also times when you have said, *"Why didn't I do that? I knew I should have...."*

You see, often you'll have a cool idea, you think about it, and maybe even tell someone about it. But you don't go ahead with the idea because your mind gets into the act. *"You can't do that." "It won't work." "You'll look foolish." "It will take too long."* And guess what? You talk yourself out of it. Only afterwards, when someone else does something with that idea, do you say, *"Man, I knew I should have...."*

Don't get me wrong. We need our mind. But it can get out of control and take us into some really dangerous territory. And often it plays the same record over and over again.

But wait—ultimately, who is in charge of your mind? **YOU ARE.**

So which is right, that core 'knowing' that you were awesome or the thoughts racing around in your mind?

Watch out, your mind will kick in again: "But I mess up. I'm not really that good. If people really knew me, they would see all my flaws."

The fact is, your intuition does know the truth—that underneath your actions and your insecurities and your worries, you are a perfectly wonderful, imperfect human being.

What else do you expect to be—an elephant?

Relax. Respect yourself. When you do this, you will find that you start making those choices that reflect your higher self, the real you. You won't be as easily influenced by others or by what you think you **NEED.** You will live from that calm, deep, peaceful **YOU** that doesn't get thrashed around by other people and events in the world.

You will do what's truly best for you. And it will be good.

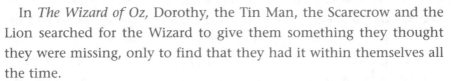

Sometimes we think that the best information is out there somewhere—in books, on the Internet, in libraries, or with our superiors, or authorities in the field. But the best information about you lies within you. The answers to your questions about what is best for you, what your talents are, what direction you should head, what is safe and what isn't—these answers are within you.

YOU are the expert on you! Listen to Your Inner Compass.

In *The Wizard of Oz*, Dorothy, the Tin Man, the Scarecrow and the Lion searched for the Wizard to give them something they thought they were missing, only to find that they had it within themselves all the time.

We are the same way. We think that our life would be better if we were smarter, richer, funnier, prettier, taller, skinnier, etc. But we already have all we need to make our life better—we just need to recognize and honor it.

Remember:

**"Oz never did give nothing to the Tin Man
That he didn't...didn't already have."**

— *Dewey Bunnell, in the song "Tin Man" by America ©1974*

BE THANKFUL

Be thankful that you don't already have everything you desire.
If you did, what would there be to look forward to?
Be thankful when you don't know something,
For it gives you the opportunity to learn.

Be thankful for the difficult times.
During those times you grow.
Be thankful for your limitations,
Because they give you opportunities for improvement.
Be thankful for each new challenge,
Because it will build your strength and character.

Be thankful for your mistakes.
They will teach you valuable lessons.
Be thankful when you're tired and weary,
Because it means you've made a difference.

It's easy to be thankful for the good things.
A life of rich fulfillment comes to those who are
also thankful for the setbacks.
Gratitude can turn a negative into a positive.
Find a way to be thankful for your troubles,
And they can become your blessings.

Author Unknown

Tools for the Road:

Tips and Ideas to Help Along the Way

With every experience, you alone are painting your own canvas, thought-by-thought, choice-by-choice.

Oprah Winfrey, Entertainment Executive, Talk Show Host, Magazine Publisher, and Actress

If you don't like something, change it.
If you can't change it, change your attitude. Don't complain.

Maya Angelou, Author and Poet (1928–)

If you are distressed by anything external,
the pain is not due to the thing itself, but to your estimate of it;
and this you have the power to revoke at any moment.

Marcus Aurelius Antoninus, Roman Emperor (121 A.D.–180 A.D.)

To drift is to be in hell, to be in heaven is to steer.

George Bernard Shaw, Irish Dramatist and Socialist (1856–1950)

Destiny...is not a matter of chance, it is a matter of choice;
it is not a thing to be waited for, it is a thing to be achieved.

William Jennings Bryan, U.S. Lawyer, Orator, and Politician (1860–1925)

The world is a great mirror. It reflects back to you what you are.
If you are loving, if you are friendly, if you are helpful,
the world will prove loving and friendly and helpful to you.
The world is what you are.

Thomas Dreier, Author, Editor, and Philanthropist (1884–1976)

9

A Look in the Mirror

Just as we may look outside of ourself for our answers, we often look outside of ourself when we want our life to improve. We may think we will be happier when we get a certain job, or get out of school, or get a new car. We think our life will improve when other people treat us better, or when a certain someone says they like or love us. We may look to honors and awards or to a perceived gain in status for our sense of value. We may even blame others or events for our struggles and unhappy feelings. But to paraphrase a line from the song *"Man In The Mirror," written and composed by Siedah Garrett and Glen Ballard (1987),* If YOU want to make YOUR world a better place, take a look at YOURSELF and then make a change.

Double-Sided Mirror

You have your own thoughts and feelings, which reflect you. And another person has their own thoughts and feelings, which reflect them. So if you held a double-sided mirror between yourself and this other person, you would see yourself on your side of the mirror and they would see themselves on their side. Your side reflects what you look like but it also reflects the whole of you: your thoughts, feelings, attitudes, and the way you handle life. The other person's side of the mirror reflects what they look like, but it also reflects the whole of them: their thoughts, feelings, attitudes, and the way they handle life.

So if someone yells at you, their yelling is reflected on their side of the mirror. Their yelling reflects them. It reflects how they think and feel, and how they handle difficulties in their life. It doesn't reflect you at all. It's not about you. It's all about them.

Now, if you yell back, that reflects you—how you think and feel and how you handle difficulties.

"But wait," you say. If they are yelling at you, sure that reflects them, but then if you yell back, well, you only yelled back because they yelled at you first. Right?

> Thought is the sculptor who can create the person you want to be.
>
> *Henry David Thoreau, American Author, Poet, and Philosopher (1817–1862)*

Well, your side of the mirror reflects you, how you think, and how you handle your problems. It reflects your story.

If you say to yourself, *"Boy, that person is really in a bad mood, I wonder what happened,"* then you would probably look at them with compassion.

If you say to yourself, *"Why are they doing this to me? Who's looking? This is embarrassing,"* then you may want to slink away and hide.

If you say to yourself, *"How dare they treat me like this? Who do they think they are? I'll show them,"* then you might yell back at them.

> Everything can be taken from a man but one thing; the last of the human freedoms–to choose one's attitude in any given set of circumstances, to choose one's own way.
>
> *Viktor Emil Frankl,*
> *Austrian Neurologist,*
> *Psychiatrist, and Holocaust*
> *Survivor (1905–1997)*

The way you think about and choose to handle this situation reflects you—your thoughts, your feelings, your attitude.

Your actions reflect you, no matter what other people do.

Let's go back to this other person. Let's say they yelled at you because you ripped their new jacket. You don't expect them to be happy, right?

But wait. Their actions still reflect them. It reflects the story they told themselves.

If this other person thought, *"Well it's not the end of the world. It's only a jacket. It can be fixed,"* then they may react calmly.

If they thought, *"What a jerk! They should be more careful. How would they like it if I ripped their things,"* then they may yell at you or even worse.

Their actions reflect them, no matter what you do.

SOME EXAMPLES

*P*retend you are holding up a double-sided mirror and yelled, *"You are stupid, ugly, and worthless."* (Of course, if you were really to yell that at someone, who would that reflect?)

Now imagine the person on the other side of the mirror is Martin Luther King.

What might be happening on his side of the mirror?
What do you think he would think?
How do you think he would feel?
How do you think he would react?

Whatever is happening on his side of the mirror reflects him. You did not cause it. You did not make him feel or do anything. Whatever happens on his side of the mirror reflects his thoughts, his attitudes, and the way he handles his life.

Now pretend you yelled those same words at Mother Teresa. Mother Teresa practiced and spoke of respect for all and worked to care for some of the world's poorest people, so how do you think she would react?

Or the Dalai Lama? As the spiritual leader of Tibetan Buddhism, he preaches and practices under-standing and compassion. That's probably how he would handle this situation too.

Or Nelson Mandela, who after being unjustly imprisoned for 18 years, forgave his captors and peacefully propelled the government of South Africa towards racial respect and social equality. What do you think he would do?

Or Mahatma Gandhi, who led a nonviolent revolu-tion that resulted in India gaining freedom from Great Britain. Do you think he would react with anger?

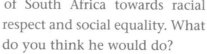

These people's thoughts, feelings, and reactions reflect what's going on inside them and how they handle life. And since these are peaceful and empowered people, they would most likely handle conflict with a peaceful attitude. They would not give away their power. They would not let you affect how they thought or acted. They would continue to act the way they wanted no matter what you said or did. Their actions would reflect their inner peace and power.

Now imagine you yelled these same words at a neighbor, a co-worker, or a family member.

What do you think they would choose to think?
How do you think they would choose to feel?
How do you think they would choose to react?

They could react thousands of different ways. How they react is based on what they think, their attitude, and the way they handle problems.

Most of us aren't as peaceful and empowered as Martin Luther King, Mother Teresa, the Dalai Lama, Nelson Mandela, or Mahatma Gandhi. Most of us give away power over our feelings and actions all the time. We let other people's behavior affect how we feel and act. And other people let our behavior affect how they feel and act. Because people often give away power over their being, your actions usually affect how people act towards you.

> A loving person lives in a loving world. A hostile person lives in a hostile world. Everyone you meet is your mirror.
>
> *Ken Keyes, Jr., Personal Growth Author and Lecturer (1921–1995)*

But in truth, each of us is responsible for our own feelings, actions, reactions, attitudes, and thoughts. We are responsible even if we choose to give away this power.

Each of us is responsible for our own side of the mirror.

Can you think of anyone in your life who frequently handles problems in a calm, peaceful manner?

Can you think of anyone in your life who frequently handles problems in an angry, vindictive manner?

A STORY OF EMPOWERMENT

While walking to a gathering, I began to think about Tracy. Tracy was going to be there, and I didn't particularly like to be around her. She talks about others. She makes fun of people and puts them down. If she doesn't like you, she will say so behind your back. I began to wonder if she liked me or if she talked about me when I wasn't around. I wondered if she made fun of my mistakes.

Then all of a sudden I stopped. I remembered the double-sided mirror.

Tracy talks about people. That reflects Tracy.

Tracy makes fun of people and laughs at their mistakes. That reflects Tracy.

Tracy may talk about me when I'm not around. But guess what? I'm not there so I don't know it. And even if she does, that reflects Tracy.

Then I thought about my side of the mirror. I like myself. I like who I am. And if Tracy doesn't like me, well, that's just too bad—that's her loss. You know, as much as I would like for everyone to like me, that's just not going to happen. And I can live with that.

I realized I was spending a lot of time thinking about Tracy, worrying about what was on her side of the mirror. I can't change Tracy, but I can change me. I can change my thoughts.

I don't have to spend any more time worrying about Tracy. I can focus on my side of the mirror instead. Besides, I like what's on my side and that's all that really matters.

So I went to the gathering and I didn't pay much attention to what Tracy said or did that day. I had a great time. Tracy didn't change; I DID. I changed the way I thought. And when I changed my thoughts, I changed my life.

Think of it like a scale.

When your side is high, the other side is low.

When your confidence is high and you are 'up' on yourself, you worry very little about what Tracy or anyone else thinks. You give them very little time in your mind. What they say or do is of little importance to you. You pay little attention to them.

When your side is low, the other side is high.

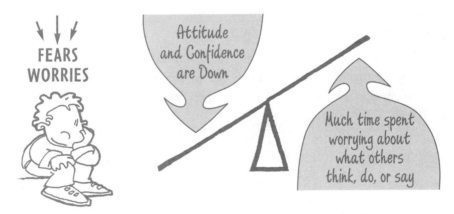

But when you're weighed down with fears and worries and your confidence is low, you worry a lot about what other people think. You give them a lot of time in your mind. You make a big deal out of what they say and what you perceive is their attitude towards you. You pay a lot of attention to them.

When you like yourself, your confidence is high. You focus on your side of the mirror and stop wasting time and energy worrying about what happens on the other side.

So where does confidence come from?

It comes from within you. It comes from your side of the mirror. It comes from what you say to yourself about yourself. If others put you down or criticize you, that reflects their side of the mirror and who they are. And if you listen to them and accept their assessment of you, then you have adopted their vision.

> Perhaps the most valuable lesson of life is to learn to make yourself do the thing you have to do, when it ought to be done, whether you like it or not (altered).
> *Thomas H. Huxley,*
> *English Biologist (1825–1895)*

But you choose who and what you listen to and who and what you believe. Confidence comes from what you say to yourself, not from what others say to you or about you.

And if you say, *"But I don't like what's on my side of the mirror,"* ask yourself this:

How did you develop this assessment of yourself? Would Martin Luther King, Mother Teresa, or the Dalai Lama think that way about you too? What thoughts are you allowing to spin around in your head? What feelings are whirling around in your being? Are you going to continue to let them spin, or are you going to question them and let them go?

It's your choice. It's your life.

You choose who and what you think about.
You choose how you interpret what you see.
You choose how you view others and your life.
You choose how much time you give things in your mind.

You choose how your life goes. You are POWERFUL.

Observe, Don't Absorb

So what happens when other people treat you poorly, when they are mean or cruel, or do things intended to hurt? What should you do? How should you handle it? Chapter 13 of this book will offer more suggestions, but here is a way to view this problem.

You can either **Observe** or **Absorb** their negative energy.

If you **Observe**, you watch them like you are looking at them through a lens or a window. You see the pain they are demonstrating, and you may even feel for them (empathize with them) and/or try to understand, but their pain doesn't become part of you.

Or you could be like a sponge and **Absorb** their negative energy, feel it, be hurt by it, have it become a part of you. If you absorb this negative energy, you will now have those negative feelings within you, causing you pain. You might then turn around and share some of this negativity with others.

When we take things personally, we absorb and we think the negative things are about us. But another person's actions and feelings are never about us. Their actions and feelings are about them. Their actions and feelings reflect how they have learned to handle life.

So if someone yells at you, puts you down, tries to make you feel inferior or guilty, just watch him or her. You can watch with curiosity, or wonder, or even caring concern, but don't absorb the feeling they are sending your way. That's theirs. Look at them through a lens; don't be a sponge.

A communications process called Nonviolent Communication (http://www.cnvc.org) emphasizes that a person's words and actions reflect their feelings and needs. So as you watch and listen to this person, try to look past their actions to see what feelings and needs they are expressing. If you observe, you just watch, without judgment or blame. You watch to try to understand. But you don't absorb their turbulence. Their actions tell about them, not you.

✦✦ SYMPATHY OR EMPATHY

But what if a friend is pouring out their heart and soul to you? Should you observe or absorb?

Well, if you absorb their pain, now instead of one person being devastated, there are two. Empathize with them, try to understand what it feels like for them, but don't share the feeling with them. This is the difference between empathy and sympathy. Empathy tries to understand and feel 'for' another. Sympathy involves taking on the other's feelings. Sympathy is like jumping into a whirlpool with the other person. Now you are both spinning around and around. Empathy stays to the side, listens, tries to understand and help, but doesn't jump in and spin.

Once I was feeling sad for a friend because he was going through a rough time. Then I realized, my feeling sad wasn't helping him, and it wasn't helping me either. So I worked at letting this feeling go. I focused on positive appreciative thoughts and sent him a message of hope instead. This helped me, and I believe it helped him.

A Wise Use of Your Time

You could spend a lot of time trying to figure out why people act the way they do. But is that a wise use of your time? Heck, it's hard enough to figure yourself out, let alone another person. And even trying to figure yourself out may not be the best use of your time. Learning to let go of negative feelings and thoughts and focus instead on positive, grateful feelings and thoughts works best to help you improve your life. When you learn to feel better, many of your problems seem to melt away. Would you rather look back to analyze the past or figure out how to move forward? Use your time wisely.

Happiness – an Inside Job

I want to be happy. I want to feel love. Don't we all!

Susie is spinning and twirling…just feeling good and enjoying herself. All of a sudden she looks up and notices people watching and smiling. So she twirls some more. But now, instead of just spinning for the sheer joy of it, she watches others for their reaction. If they keep smiling she feels happy and does it more. If they start frowning or give her mean looks, she may feel bad and stop. She has gone from just enjoying herself for herself to watching others to see how she should feel about herself.

From an early age many of us learn to watch others to see how we should feel about ourselves. If people treated us as special and wonderful, we probably felt special and wonderful. But if they treated us as if we were bad, dumb, or undesirable, then we may have thought we were bad, dumb, or undesirable too. We often adopted their view of us. So did the other people really 'cause' our beliefs and feelings? Did we just blindly accept their assessment? And now that we are older and realize other people's actions reflect them, can we change our assessment if we want?

If you did adopt someone else's negative assessment of you, don't be too hard on yourself. You probably learned this at a very young age.

When Jake was a baby, his mom and dad were often angry at each other. But Jake didn't know this. He just knew that they were angry. When he was really young and they would argue, Jake would cry and want to be held. His dad would get mad and tell him to stop crying. Then his mom would yell at his dad. Jake thought HE CAUSED them to argue. (That's a lot of power for a little kid to think they have, and it can feel scary.) Jake often felt unwanted and unloved. He began to think he was a bad person. And although he tried to please his parents, somewhere, sometime he would goof up (just like everyone will), and they would get mad and yell at him. He grew up watching others to see how they responded to him. If the response was positive, he thought he was okay, but when the response was negative, he felt down or angry.

Sometimes people like Jake get so hurt and discouraged that they give up trying. They say, "What the heck. I'm just a bad person anyway. Why even try?" And then you and I, and schools and society, have to deal with the end result.

Choosing for yourself

But now you are older and can use your Thinking Brain to see and understand what is happening. You can begin to see that another person's actions reflect them and don't say a thing about you. You can learn to let go of all those old negative lessons you picked up along the way. You can begin to develop your own perspective of yourself and your value, regardless of how others treat you or what others say. You can learn to accept and love yourself with your strength and your struggles and stop looking to others for how to feel about yourself. You are that powerful!

You can begin to realize that you are fine on your side of the mirror. You are not perfect, but you are perfectly human.

Your feelings are within you. You create them by the way you think. Susie had positive feelings when she was first spinning, before she looked to others to validate them. Now when she looks at others, she can keep those positive feelings no matter what looks she gets or what others might say. Happiness is an inside job, dependent upon you and your thoughts. And you don't NEED someone else to love you for you to feel love.

Here is another way to look at it. Let's say you are 'in love' with someone who doesn't even know you exist. It could be a rock or movie star, or someone who just walked by, or someone you saw at a party. Now, how does it feel to be 'in love' with this person? You get excited just thinking about them. Your heart beats faster. You feel energized. You skip around with a smile on your face and feel wonderful.

Now where are these feelings coming from? They aren't coming from the other person. They don't even know you exist. These feelings are coming from within you. You are creating these wonderful, energetic, positive feelings. You are the one feeling love, excitement, and wonderful, and you are doing it all by yourself. Every time you look and think about this other person you may think they have caused these feelings within you, but how could they have caused them? They don't even know you. It's your own thoughts that have caused these feelings.

So it's not others that create a feeling within you. You create it within you. And you can learn to create it within you no matter what others say or do.

Sure it helps if others treat you in positive ways, but other people's actions and attitudes towards you are not prerequisites for those good feelings. Just like Susie, we have often learned to stop looking within ourselves for those positive feelings and have instead relied on others for our own sense of well-being. But remember, other people's actions and attitudes towards you reflect them, how they see themselves, what they think they need. It's not about you at all.

Happiness, pride, love, and acceptance don't come from outside; they come from within. These good feelings come from what you say to yourself about yourself. But so do negative feelings like hurt, shame, embarrassment, anger, and sadness.

It reminds me of the song by Country/Western singer Waylon Jennings:

"Looking for love in all the wrong places
Looking for love in too many faces
Searching your eyes, looking for traces
Of what...I'm dreaming of..."

Often we look for someone else to love us, to treat us as important and special. But aren't we looking in the wrong place for these special feelings? Sure, you may find someone out there to send you these messages, but if you think that the reason you feel love is because of them, aren't you saying they basically control your feelings? Do you really want to leave your happiness and sense of importance in someone else's hands? Does this feel strong or weak?

Stop looking outside of yourself for the good feelings about yourself. Look no further than the person in the mirror. You see, love and happiness are **INSIDE** jobs.

Conditional vs. Unconditional Love–The Difference

Some people communicate, either through their words or actions, that they love you only when:

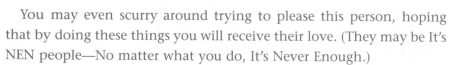

...you do what they want
...you look pretty or handsome
...they are proud of you
...they are in a good mood
...you wait on them
...you buy them things
...you do this or that for them

You may even scurry around trying to please this person, hoping that by doing these things you will receive their love. (They may be It's NEN people—No matter what you do, It's Never Enough.)

But these are conditions and this is conditional love. These people share their love only when certain conditions are met. But what about other times?

Sometimes we even put conditions on the love we feel for ourselves.

I will be happy with myself (I would love myself):
...when I lose weight
...when I get better at...
...when I win
...if I were prettier

Conditional love is based on judgment. Someone decides whether you are lovable or not. Even you may decide whether you are lovable or not. Conditional love is unstable. It fluctuates depending upon this judgment.

Unconditional love is always there. You don't have to do anything, be any way, or prove anything to receive this love. It doesn't fluctuate. There is no judgment or conditions. You are lovable just as you are.

Unconditional love is true love.

SELF-CONFIDENCE ≠ ARROGANCE

These feelings of acceptance, importance, and love are not about being superior to others; they are about feelings and beliefs about you. I once heard someone say that the problem with today's youth is that they had too much self-esteem; they thought they were better than others. If a person thinks they are more important than others, that's arrogance, not self-esteem. Look around you; you know the difference. Think of someone you know who is comfortable and confident within themselves. Now think of someone who acts like she is better than others. Now which person seem more at peace with themselves and life?

Look in the Mirror

When looking for love or confidence, look in the mirror and focus on yourself. Once you create positive feelings within yourself, you will radiate them out to the world. And as you radiate them out to the world, you become like a magnet, attracting these same feelings back to you. Your love and happiness starts with you.

Life is like a ten-speed bike.
Most of us have gears we never use.

Charles Schultz, Cartoonist (1922–2000)

There is no failure except in no longer trying.

Elbert Hubbard, Author, Publisher, and Lecturer (1856–1915)

Every day is an opportunity to make your
life the way you want it to be. Anything is possible
when you work toward it, one day at a time.

Ralph Marston, Writer and Publisher (1955–)

The future doesn't lie ahead of you, waiting to happen....
It lies deep inside of you waiting to be discovered.

Anonymous

You might not be able to control everything that
happens to you, but you can control what you do about it.

Dr. Phil McGraw, Psychologist, Author, and Talk Show Host (1950–)

Do not let what you cannot do interfere
with what you can do.

John Wooden, Basketball Coach (1910–)

10

Traveling Tips and Tools

Stories and Analogies For the Road of Life ✛

Soup

A *re your thoughts mostly positive, accepting, and respectful—or negative,*
critical, and judgmental?

And how did the thoughts get there?

Well, that's a good question. And there is not just one easy answer.
Actually, think of it like soup.

You start with a basic broth—your own temperament style—then
you add lots of ingredients, like your experiences and interactions with
others. How it all mixes together determines the way you think. So
everyone's soup is different.

The basic broth

Every one of us is born with a core personality style. It's called our temperament. It's noticeable in newborns. Some infants are calm and joyful, while others are intense and irritable. Some babies are immediately drawn to new stimuli, and others need more time to warm up and may even pull back in fear. Some infants sit quietly and seem to entertain themselves for hours. Others are constantly on the move and jump from one thing to another. Your temperament is the base broth of your thinking style. It's there from birth and affects the taste of everything else that is added (see *Temperament Styles* below).

✦ ✦ TEMPERAMENT STYLES

Research by psychiatrists Stella Chess and Alexander Thomas identified nine temperament traits that parents could no more change than they could change the color of their child's eyes.

1. **ACTIVITY LEVEL:** how much a child moves about and how often the child is active.

2. **REGULARITY:** how predictable a child is in body functions, such as hunger, sleep, and bowel movements.

3. **APPROACH/WITHDRAWAL:** the way a child first reacts to a new situation or thing—a new food, toy, person, or place.

4. **ADAPTABILITY:** how a child responds over the long-term in new or different situations. How easy is it to get the child to change?

5. **PHYSICAL SENSITIVITY:** how strong something has to be to get a reaction to touch, taste, smell, texture, or sound.

(continues on next page)

(continued from previous page)

6. **QUALITY of MOOD:** the amount of pleasant, friendly, and happy behavior compared with the amount of grouchy, solemn, or unhappy behavior.

7. **INTENSITY of REACTIONS:** the energy level of response, positive or negative.

8. **DISTRACTIBILITY:** how easily something draws the child's attention away from something he/she is doing.

9. **PERSISTENCE and ATTENTION SPAN:** These go together. Persistence is how long a child keeps working on something even when it's difficult, and attention span is how long the child does something without stopping.

Each child is a combination of these different styles. A high-activity/irregular/low-adaptability child would be more difficult to raise than a low-activity/regular/very adaptable child.

Look through these style categories and think about yourself. From the stories you have heard, how do you think you were as a child? How would you now rate yourself in each of these areas? Although we can change as we develop and learn, our core temperament is the base from where we start and can remain fairly consistent throughout life.

Added ingredients (experiences) to your soup

Sometimes things happen that have a big impact in your life, such as having an older sibling who treated you as special or was cruel; being attacked by an animal; being abused; losing someone close to you; moving frequently; or living with parents who argued often or even divorced. As an infant you watched the people in your environment. How did they handle their feelings, their relationships, or adversity? You watched and learned. All of these ingredients affect your soup—the way you think.

The experiences that have the most impact on the flavor of your soup are your interactions with others, especially your family. Did people treat you as special or unimportant, wanted or a burden? Did someone label you as smart, dumb, good, bad, lazy, too wild, pretty, ugly? Did someone say you were uncoordinated, couldn't sing, couldn't dance, weren't as good as or were better than others in some area? What type of messages did you receive from the people in your environment?

All your life, other people have tried to add to your mix through their words or actions. They tried to tell you how you should view yourself and your world. Did you listen to them and add these ingredients to your soup? Did you add just a little dash, or did you pour it in?

But aren't these just other human beings with their own perceptions of life and how life should be? Their opinions reflect them—they aren't law, unless we allow them to be.

> What you have to do and the way you have to do it is incredibly simple. Whether you are willing to do it, that's another matter.
>
> *Peter Drucker, US (Austrian-born) Business Management Professor and Author (1909–2005)*

Some experiences and interactions add little to your soup, while others alter the taste dramatically. As a little kid you just did what came naturally (based upon your temperament—your soup broth). Some kids just naturally don't add the negative stuff to their soup, while others seem to pick up everything that is tossed their way. And once these thoughts, impressions, and ideas have been added, they become part of you. You may not even remember where the feeling or idea came from. It's just part of your soup now.

The nice thing about this soup is that we can continually adjust the taste. We can toss out those ingredients (beliefs, thoughts) that don't help us feel good and add new ones that do. And with work, we can even alter the broth. We have control over our mix.

The people we are closest to have the most influence on our soup mix. Since our family, especially our parents, contribute much to the way we view ourselves and our world, here is another analogy that might help you understand how you got to be who you are.

Family Baggage

Even before you were born, you sensed emotions. You sensed whether people were happy, anxious, angry, peaceful, or sad. You felt it in your mother's body, and you heard it in the tones of people's voices. Once you were born you continued to sense your world. Did you feel safe? Did people care for you, or did you feel like a burden? Was your world predictable, or did you feel unsure? You watched the people in your family. How did they interact? Were they respectful or was there continual conflict? How did they handle struggles? Did they fight life or bounce back from difficulties? Did they communicate hopelessness, anger, or a defeatist attitude? Or was their message one of optimism with a take-charge and a can-do attitude? Their relationship patterns and attitudes toward life spilled over to affect how they treated you.

Positive feelings were warm, safe, and happy. Respectful interaction patterns led to comfortable relationships. Optimistic, can-do attitudes felt strong, and you sensed that people had power over their lives. And if this is primarily what you picked up from your family, then life is good.

But what if instead you encountered and absorbed negative patterns and attitudes? Those negative feelings become fears and worries stored somewhere in your body. Judgmental and critical interaction patterns led to relationships that involved much turmoil. Negative, pessimistic, helpless attitudes made you feel weak and not in control. Nervous and uptight approaches led to a fearful view of life. And if you now carry these negative feelings, model these disrespectful interactions, or have adopted this pessimistic or fearful attitude towards life, this becomes your baggage.

The baggage stays there until you bring it forward, open it, examine it, and work at letting it go. But we don't want to examine some of the baggage because first, it contains negative feelings that are scary, and second, it means we would have to work at changing long-term patterns. So instead we carry this baggage around, letting it weigh us down.

But wait, where did this baggage come from anyway? Your parents. And now you're carrying this baggage. How unfair.

So that means your parents have baggage too, because they have to have it in order to pass it on to you.

So, where did your parents get their baggage?

Well, they were once unborn babies who heard voices and could sense tones, and once they were born they watched behavior patterns.... Oh, you know this story. So your parents got some of their baggage from their parents—your grandparents. And now your parents are sharing it with you. (Most people don't intentionally pass on their baggage. In fact they often say, "I'm not going to be like my parents." But then they feel stressed or they don't know what else to do, and they end up carrying the same baggage.)

So that means your grandparents had baggage too.

And where did your grandparents get some of their baggage? Well, once they were unborn babies.... It's the same old story. They got it from their parents—your great-grandparents.

And where did your great-grandparents get their baggage?

Well, the rest is just history.

So we're just passing some of our family baggage on and on from generation to generation UNTIL someone gets the courage and takes the effort to open up the bags, decides that what's inside isn't worth carrying around, and works at letting that old useless baggage go.

What baggage did you pick up from your family?

Maybe you will be the one to stop carrying this baggage and passing it on.

Remember the safe, happy feelings, the optimism, and the respect, and let the baggage go. It's of no use to you anyway. ***Let it go!***

Now remember, we didn't get all of our baggage from our parents; some came from others we connected with, and some we created all by ourselves. Baggage can come from all kinds of territories.

A FAMILY WITHOUT BAGGAGE–
What It Would (and Wouldn't) Look Like

So what if you were born into a family that didn't have baggage? What might that look like?

◆ For one, you would ALWAYS feel valued and loved. There would never be a time when you questioned this! NEVER!

◆ There would be no hitting, yelling, cold shoulders, silent treatments, evil looks, distance, guilt trips, foul talk, berating, criticism, etc.

◆ There would be hugs, respect, comfort, peace, open communication, acceptance, understanding, etc., and, of course, you would be treated the same way in private as you were in public.

◆ You would always know that you are good enough just as you are. You wouldn't have to keep proving your worth.

◆ You would not be held responsible for someone else's sense of value, happiness, or actions. That is their side of the mirror.

◆ When you made a mistake (which you would because you are human) it would be dealt with in a calm, loving manner, with natural consequences. It would be treated as a learning experience to help you grow rather than another opportunity to knock you down.

If you were born into a family with some baggage, as most of us were, YOU DID NOT CREATE THE BAGGAGE. It was there LONG before you were born. You are not responsible for your parents' baggage! And, you cannot MAKE your parents or others feel happy, loved, important, special, or valued. You can't MAKE people disagree or fight. How people handle their problems is based upon what they have learned and how they choose to think and feel. You are responsible for only your own thoughts and feelings and for the messages you send to others. So work on your own baggage and let it go so the messages you send forward are ones of peace, acceptance, and love.

Everyone Has Some Baggage

Every person has their own set of struggles, their own set of baggage. We have no idea what it has been like to be another person. We don't know their thoughts, their worries, or their fears. We don't have their exact temperament, and we have not lived their life from zero to now. People are doing the best they can at that moment. If they could do better, don't you think they would?

We are the same way. Sometimes we know what to do, but we just can't get ourselves to do it. Our habits of thinking and behaving are often so set that we keep falling into the same patterns over and over, even though we know better. Remember, when we are stressed, we

often stop using our Thinking Brain and rely on our Survival Brain and Emotional Brain. These two react without much thought; they react with patterns of the past. It's like a rut in a muddy road. When we stop using our Thinking Brain, we slip right back into the rut, into the grooves of the past.

But remember, each of us is doing the best we can at each moment of our life.

To judge others you must see yourself as superior, above them. But you aren't. You are just another human being, with your own set of struggles. You have your own lessons in life. We are all works in-progress, like unfinished works of art. Honor and respect each person's struggle, especially your own.

> If we could read the secret history of our enemies, we should find in each man's life sorrow and suffering enough to disarm any hostility.
>
> *Henry Wadsworth Longfellow, American Poet (1807–1882)*

Mountains

How big do you make your problems?

Have you heard the saying, "Don't make a mountain out of a mole-hill?" Well, problems come in different sizes. There are mountain sized problems and molehill sized problems. How you think affects the size of your problem.

If you think: *This is TERRIBLE, HORRIBLE, WHY DID THIS HAPPEN TO ME?* or if you DEMAND that things go the way you want, then you create a MOUNTAIN out of your problem. Instead of moving quickly beyond this problem, you waste a lot of time and energy. And if you keep thinking that way, you create even more mountains in the future.

But if you think: *This is no big deal. I can handle this. I'll be okay,* then your problem will be like a hill or even a little pebble in your path you hardly notice. You move right past it and continue on your journey. And later, you may not even remember it.

(Baggage makes any travel more difficult because it weighs you down. The lighter your load, the easier your travel.)

Even when you have mountain sized problems, how you think determines the path you take to get through them. If you focus on how terrible and unfair the problem is, then you have picked a difficult path and you will probably create even more mountains.

Instead, you can focus on what you can do to make things better. Focus on little steps you can take instead of trying to scale the whole mountain at one time. Ask yourself what life lessons you can gain from this experience. No matter how bad life is, you can find some positives. And if you choose to do this, you will create an easier path to travel.

As Adrienne E. Gusoff, Humorist, Writer, and Entertainer (1953–) once said, "Not only is life a bitch, it has puppies." So if your life is full of mountains, even the easiest path may be difficult.

But no matter how difficult your path, you have choices.

The choices you make determine whether your life is miserable or you find some happiness.

TRUE SURVIVORS

*P*eople who struggle in life often blame their struggles on things that have happened to them or 'been done to' them.

My mother was an alcoholic, my dad was never there for me, I was abused, the teachers didn't like me, people picked on me, yada yada yada.

The list of bad things that have happened in your past could go on and on. But the truth is, it doesn't matter what happened in your past, it matters what happens in your head. No matter what you can point to, there is someone else who has experienced similar problems and is not only surviving, but is actually thriving. Here are some of their stories.

In 2003, a shark attacked 13 year old Bethany Hamilton, an expert surfer planning to turn pro. She lost her left arm but not her spirit. Within weeks of surgery to seal the wound, Bethany was surfing again. Bethany now surfs professionally and has won numerous awards and contests. She was selected for the 2005 USA Surf Team, and won her first national surfing title that same year.

Dave Pelzer experienced extreme abuse from his mentally disturbed, alcoholic mother. He was hit, kicked, burned, starved, and locked in the basement. Finally, at the age of twelve, Dave was rescued and placed in a foster home. After all this, Dave rebelled and got in trouble at school and with the law. After moving through five foster homes, Dave finally realized that if he didn't change, he would spend the rest of his life in and out of trouble. From that point on, Dave worked to create a life with meaning. Dave writes and speaks about his experiences. His first book, A Child Called "IT" was on the New York Times Best Sellers List for over six years. Through his actions, Dave demonstrated resiliency and showed all that when you take personal responsibility for your life, anyone can overcome adversity.

(continues on next page)

(continued from previous page)

Benjamin Solomon Carson and his brother were raised in poverty. Their mother, who had married at 13 and divorced when Ben was 8, worked two and sometimes three jobs just to get by. By the time Ben was 9, he was at the bottom of his class and described himself as the "class dummy." That's when his mother turned off the TV and required her sons to read and write a report on two books a week. His mother would study the reports and give encouragement. Later, Ben learned that his third-grade educated mother hadn't even been able to read the reports. As a result of this work, Ben slowly worked his way to the top of his class. He was awarded a scholarship to Yale and went on to study medicine at the University of Michigan. Benjamin Carson is now the Director of the Division of Pediatric Neurosurgery at Johns Hopkins. Not bad for the "class dummy."

Mary Groda-Lewis had many strikes against her. Her family was poor and often worked as migrant workers. One year she attended five different schools. Mary struggled academically, was labeled 'retarded,' and at a young age she dropped out of school. As a teenager, she rebelled, got in trouble,and spent years in reformatories. There, she finally learned to read and write. By 19, an unwed Mary had two children. But that's not all. During the birth of her second child, she suffered cardiac arrest, seizures, and a stroke. She had to learn to walk and talk all over again. Once she recovered, she started attending college and finally graduated at the age of 29. Then she decided she wanted to become a doctor. But because of her educational background, she had difficulty finding a medical school that would accept her. Finally she was accepted at one school. She struggled during her first year in medical school and, as she had done many times before, she questioned whether she was smart enough or good enough to go on. But go on she did, and at the age of 35 she graduated from medical school and is now practicing medicine in Hawaii.

Are You a Survivor?

So what is the difference between being a Survivor and seeing yourself as a Victim?

◆ Survivors focus on what they can do. Victims focus on what has been done to them.

◆ Survivors are optimistic. Victims are pessimistic.

◆ Survivors take control of their lives. Victims believe their lives are out of their control.

> One of the secrets of life is to make stepping-stones out of stumbling blocks.
>
> *Jack Penn, Surgeon and Author (1909–1996)*

◆ Survivors use time and energy to do what needs to be done so that they can move forward. Victims use time and energy to look back, complain, or feel sorry for themselves.

◆ Survivors look inside to find their strength and direction. Victims look outside for excuses and for someone or something to blame.

◆ Survivors keep going and trying. Victims give up.

As an old Japanese proverb goes, *"Fall seven times. Stand up eight."*

Are you still standing?

I Can't Go On–I Have a Mountain Problem

What if you have a mountain problem? What if your world seems to be coming apart at the seams?

The love of your life left or died.

Everyone you know has turned against you.

You lose your home or possessions.

You totally blew a huge opportunity.

You are humiliated in front of the world (or at least your world).

Life just isn't going the way you want at all.

If you were to rate problems from one to ten (ten being the most difficult) you see your problem as a **GIANT TEN.**

But who decided it was a ten? What thoughts created this belief? Where are those thoughts? No matter how big or devastating the events in your life, you choose how you think and act, which then determines how long it will take to get past this major obstacle.

When we allow ourselves to get stuck in a problem, we are **STANDING TOO CLOSE**.

The closer we stand, the more our problems dominate our view. They look overwhelming. We lose our perspective. We can't see a way around or a life beyond these obstacles. When we focus primarily on obstacles and our misery, we lose sight of other parts of our lives, including other people. We become self-absorbed, self-centered, self-focused.

So we get stuck and say things like:

"My life is ruined."
"I CAN'T GO ON!"
And if others try to help, we say, *"But you just don't understand."*

And that is true. Nobody truly understands HOW you are feeling and what you are thinking. Nobody understands how big this obstacle is to you. Nobody really knows because these thoughts and feelings are inside you.

But people do understand about obstacles. They have had them in their own lives and have moved on. They have seen other people overcome difficulties, so they know that you can too. And since your problem is not dominating their view, they can see alternative paths and life beyond this problem.

You may say, *"But nobody has it as bad as I do."*

Get REAL. Did you read those survivor stories? Are you still breathing? Do you have food to eat? Were you locked in a basement for days and weeks? Were you a P.O.W. who was starved and tortured? Are bombs going off near your house? Have all your neighbors been rounded up and shipped off to concentration camps? Do you live where people are dying all around you? Have you lost everything—**EVERYTHING**?

People have survived situations worse than yours.

The only reason your problem seems so bad and overwhelming is that it's YOUR PROBLEM. You are the one thinking about it, focusing on it, letting it dominate your view.

BACK UP

Back away from your problem and take a look around you. Look for things you can do to help others. Focus on other parts of your life or actions you can take to get past this problem. When you back up, you will see that there are ways around your problem and there is life on the other side. Only when you back away do you realize you can get beyond this life crisis.

When you think the world has turned its back on you,
take another look: most likely, you turned your back on the world.

Anonymous

MORE TIPS AND TOOLS

Start your climb today

Sometimes when faced with a difficulty, we avoid thinking about it and maybe even wait until the last minute to handle it. But if we wait and think about it, and wait and think about it, the problem gets bigger and bigger, and the path gets steeper and steeper. So when we finally decide to tackle this problem, the slope is steep and the climb much more difficult.

Instead of waiting and thinking, start today on your path toward solving or handling this problem. If you take little steps every day, soon you will turn around and realize how far you have gotten towards solving or moving past this problem.

A journey of a thousand miles must begin with a single step.

Chinese Proverb

How much and how long do you retell your story?

When someone is mean to you, how long does it last?
Were they mean for one minute, two, a couple of minutes each day?
When something bad happened, how long did it last?
Ten minutes, two days, two years?
And even if it lasts years, is it constant or intermittent? Are there other things in your life besides this problem?

Now the big question: How much and how long do you think about it, relive it, complain about it, and tell the story about it over and over again in your head?

How much do you let it dominate your mood, your attitude, and your life?

How long do you carry it?

So let's see...

Don yelled at you—which took about ten seconds.

You relive it, think about it over and over again for the next three weeks...three months...three years....

3 weeks later | 3 months later | 3 years later

So who has caused you more pain?

When you stay upset about something, thinking about it over and over again—you are the one who causes you pain, because you are the one who keeps telling the story. The longer you think about it, the more of a mountain you make it. (That's why forgiveness is so important.)

Remember, some people try to create mountains in other people's lives. That's how they get their sense of power. But it's your life and you decide whether you want a mountain there or not. So do what you can to change the situation. Then forgive so you can move on in your life.

(continues on next page)

(continued from previous page)

Create your own mountain chart—and chart your course

Today's problems often fade with time. So try this:

Take a sheet of paper and draw the molehill to mountain scene. Or write the word "MOUNTAIN" in large letters on the left side of the page and the word "molehill" in small letters on the right side of the page. The next time you have a problem, write a short note about it, date it, and stick it where you think it fits on this scene. Do you think it is more like a mountain problem, a molehill problem, or somewhere in the middle?

Every couple of days, look at this sheet. If you think the problem is getting bigger, move the note towards the mountain side of the chart. If you think the problem is getting smaller, move the note towards the molehill side. Some problems do get bigger, but you will notice most problems fade with time. So the next time you get all upset about something, remember, "this too shall pass."

Count Down

The next time you are upset about something ask yourself:

"Will this be a major problem in my life 100 years from now? Will it be a problem 10 years from now?...One year from now?...One month from now?"

Count it down. You can just say the numbers, "100, 10, 1..." Often, after you count a couple numbers you drop the drama and LET IT GO.

Count it down...100, 10, 1 year, 1 month, 1...

LET IT GO.

Basic Driving Tip–Keep Your Eyes on the Road

As you travel, the road of life has ups and downs, stops and starts, bumps and detours. There are so many choices to make. Which turns will you take? How will you reach your goals and dreams?

Here is a basic driving tip:

Keep your eyes on the road right in front of you.

Don't get too distracted dreaming about the future or reviewing the past. Focus on the choices you need to make right now.

If you focus too strongly on the future, thinking about how wonderful life will be when you get that new job, meet that right person, make it big, finish some schooling, etc., then you are not focusing on the choices and actions you can take right now. You are either dreaming while you are driving or looking too far ahead. You might miss a turn, get lost, hit a rut, spin your wheels, or even crash as you are stuck staring at your dream. Aim for distant goals but primarily focus on the actions you can take in the present. Look at what is around you and what you can do **RIGHT NOW**.

> Don't go around saying the world owes you a living. The world owes you nothing. It was here first.
>
> *Mark Twain, pseudonym of Samuel Langhorne Clemens, American Author, Humorist, and Social Observer (1835–1910)*

Also, don't get stuck staring into your rear view mirror, consistently rehashing or analyzing the past. You can't drive forward while you are looking backward. And forward is the only direction you can really go. What is behind you has already happened. You can't change it. Glance back to learn from it, but don't focus on it.

Life is a lesson, many lessons. So learn what you can on every road you take no matter how smooth or bumpy. And realize that some of the bumpiest roads have the most valuable lessons.

DON'T QUIT

When things go wrong, as they sometimes will,
When the road you're trudging seems all uphill,
When the funds are low and the debts are high,
And you want to smile but you have to sigh,
When care is pressing you down a bit–
Rest if you must, but don't you quit.

Life is queer with its twists and turns.
As everyone of us sometimes learns.
And many a fellow turns about
When he might have won had he stuck it out.
Don't give up though the pace seems slow
You may succeed with another blow.

Often the goal is nearer than
It seems to a faint and faltering man;
Often the struggler has given up
When he might have captured the victor's cup;
And he learned too late when the night came down,
How close he was to the golden crown.

Success is failure turned inside out–
The silver tint of the clouds of doubt,
And when you never can tell how close you are,
It may be near when it seems afar;
So stick to the fight when you're hardest hit–
It's when things seem worst, you must not quit.

When you live in reaction, you give your power away.
Then you get to experience what you gave your power to.

N. Smith (unknown)

Only those who dare to fail greatly can ever achieve greatly.

Robert F. Kennedy, Political Leader and
U.S. Attorney General (1925–1968)

If you want to make your dreams come true, wake up.
Wake up to your own strength. Wake up to the role you play
in your own destiny. Wake up to the power you have to
choose what you think, do, and say.

Keith Ellis, Motivational Speaker and Author (1953–)

Joy is not in things; it is in us.

Benjamin Franklin, American Printer, Author, Diplomat,
Philosopher, and Scientist (1706–1790)

There are powers inside of you, if you could discover and use,
[that] would make of you everything you ever dreamed or
imagined you could become.

Orison Swett Marden, Author, Publisher,
and Founder of Success Magazine (1850–1924)

I will permit no man to narrow and degrade
my soul by making me hate him.

Booker T. Washington, American Educator, Author,
and African American Leader (1856–1915)

11

More Power to You

But wait! It might be nice to have physical power. You could move items and impress people. You could stand up for and protect yourself and others. Your strength could help you develop confidence and feel proud. Those are good feelings. It might be nice to have physical power.

It might be nice to have financial power too. You could buy almost anything you wanted. You could help others. You probably wouldn't worry about starving or having a place to live. It could help you feel safe and secure. It might be nice to have financial power.

And what about social power? If you had social power, people would look up to you and want to be connected to you. This sounds nice. If you had social power you might feel confident, important, and proud. Those are good feelings.

There are benefits to having intellectual power, political power, and professional power too.

In fact if I could pick, I'd just take all of them, thank you.

But it doesn't work that way.

FEW people have ALL OF THEM!

You are dealt some talents and opportunities. You are also dealt obstacles. Then it's up to you to make the best of it all.

And how DO you make the best of it all?

How do you play your hand to create a life where you feel happy, confident, and in control?

How do you recognize your INNER POWER, and become the most POWERFUL YOU that you can be?

That's a big question. And although you have to find your own answer, here is some help:

Focus on what you can control. Make healthy choices.

Returning late at night from a long honeymoon, the couple parked and went straight to bed. They arose to find their car gone. Once they decided it wasn't a prank, they called the police and filed a report. Then they called their insurance agent and sat down to try to organize their thoughts. What a way to start a marriage. They complained and commiserated as they remembered all the gifts, clothes, and souvenirs they lost. Later that day they rented a car and tried to figure out what they were going to do with the last couple of days of their vacation. Then they made a major decision; they went shopping, and to the movies, and out with friends, and for a walk through the park. They decided to enjoy the rest of their free time together. "Besides," they said, "we couldn't do anything about the car or lost items, but we could choose how we were going to spend the rest of our vacation." They chose to have fun.

The couple was dealt obstacles. They didn't choose to have these things happen, but now they had to handle them. They could have invested a lot of time and energy into thinking and complaining about the robbery and being angry about their car, the lost items, and the hassle. But would their thinking, complaining, and being angry have made anything better? Would it have changed the robbery? Would it have brought their car back? Would it have helped solve their problem, or would it actually have made it worse? Did they really control what happened to them? Would thinking, complaining, and being angry change the situation, or would it just change the couple?

So what did the couple control? Well, they controlled themselves and their attitude, and they can control the stories they tell themselves, the thoughts they hold onto, and the ones they let go. The couple controlled how they viewed and reacted to what was dealt them. Minute-by-minute, they chose what they focused on and what they just observed and let go.

So which would have been a better use of their time: thinking, complaining, and being angry about something over which they had no control, or focusing on what they can control—their attitude and actions?

To feel happy, confident, and in control,
To recognize your POWER... Focus on what you control.
Focus on yourself, your attitude and actions, and how you live your life.

Then... Make healthy choices.

Would complaining have been a healthy choice? Would it have made anything better?

Would carrying on and on about what was lost have been a healthy choice? Would it have helped the couple get their items back, or would it have just affected their own happiness?

Healthy choices help you take your life in a positive direction. The first healthy choice the couple made was to focus on what they COULD control: themselves and their attitude. Then instead of spending more time being angry, blaming each other, regretting that they hadn't locked the car, complaining about the situation, or crying, they spent it creating new positive experiences in their life. Rather than staring backward at what had happened, they chose to look forward to what they could do. Instead of giving this unfortunate event a main chapter in their life story, they gave it a smaller part.

> There is only one way to happiness and that is to cease worrying about things which are beyond the power of our will.
>
> Epictetus, Greek Philosopher (55–135)

Instead of creating a huge pity party or fighting life, they accepted what had happened as a single event and moved on to celebrate life.

When you make healthy choices, you focus on yourself and your own thoughts. You work at creating thoughts that are optimistic, rational, and accepting. You learn to question and release thoughts that exaggerate or demand. You learn to accept life as it is, rather than expecting it to be the way you want.

◆ Yes, it was unfortunate. But, it wasn't terrible; it wasn't the end of the world.

> **When it rains, I let it.**
>
> *113-year-old man's response to a question about the secret of his longevity.*

◆ Saying people 'shouldn't' steal, or this 'shouldn't have' happened, or life 'should be' fair, would be demanding that things be a certain way. Does the couple control this? And is this type of thinking a productive use of their time? What would become of the time they spent doing this? And does demanding change anything?

◆ They could be mad at themselves or blame each other for not unpacking the car. But what good does that do? Does finding someone to blame fix the problem? Does anger towards themselves or each other make their life better? We all have regrets. The important thing is to learn from the experience and move on.

◆ They could blame the thieves for 'ruining their happiness.' But do the thieves control the couple's happiness? Who gave them that much power? Only the couple can decide how much power the thieves have in their life.

So to feel happy, confident, and in control—to recognize your inner POWER and become the most POWERFUL YOU—you can:

Focus on what you control
—and—
Make healthy choices.

YOUR POWER ZONE–
The Part of Life You Control

~~Power/Control~~	(Power/Control)

Draw a line down the middle of a piece of paper.

Write the words POWER and CONTROL at the top of the paper on both sides of this line.

Cross out these two words on the left side of the paper and circle these two words on the right side.

On the left side (the side with the words POWER and CONTROL crossed out) list some parts of life you DO NOT control. This list could include your brother, your 'special' someone, the weather, the TV news, your boss, the past, the future, your parents, etc. This is your NO POWER ZONE. Ultimately you have NO POWER over this part of life.

On the right side (the side with the words POWER and CONTROL circled) list the parts of life you DO control. This list would include YOU, your thoughts, your attitudes, and your actions. This is your POWER ZONE. This is the part of life you have POWER over, the only part you truly control.

(After making your list, look at the sample list on page 202.)

Compare the left and right sides of your list.

Which side do you mainly focus on, think about, worry about, or complain about?

Your NO POWER side, or your POWER side?

Where do you spend most of your time and energy?

For example, let's say you want someone to like you. This could be a new acquaintance, a neighbor, an employer, anybody. So how do you spend your time? You could focus on THEM, think of ways to impress THEM, and worry about what THEY think. You could spend a lot of time concentrating on THEM. But, you don't control THEM. You don't control whether they like you or what they think of you. You could be nice and friendly and helpful, but they still may not like you. So if you focus on them, you are focusing on a part of life you DO NOT control. You are focusing on your NO POWER ZONE.

Instead, let's say you focus on what you do control. You focus on YOURSELF, YOUR wanting and wishing, YOUR thoughts, attitudes, and actions. You work on being optimistic, yet rational. You remind yourself that not everyone will like you. You realize you can still have a happy life even if they don't. You realize that their attitude and actions reflect them, and it really has little or nothing to do with you. You realize that you don't control them. But that's good, because they don't control you either. You accept the fact that things don't always go the way you would like but that you can still survive. Now you are focusing on the things you DO control. You are focusing on choices you can make. You are focusing on your POWER ZONE.

SAMPLE LIST

Power/Control (crossed out)		Power/Control (circled)
parents	past	YOU!!!
friends	future	Your hands
spouses	weather	feel
other people	government	mouth
their thoughts,	schools	words
feelings,	society	actions
attitude,	bosses	effort
and actions	co-workers	attitude
hair color	trees	feelings
eye color	nature	thoughts
your basic body	traffic	what you watch on TV
shape and size	airplanes	what you participate in
what is on TV	other cars	
the outcome of events you watch		
(even the events you participate in)		
certain bodily functions		

When would you feel more powerful? When you put time and energy into things you don't control, or when you put time and energy into things you DO control?

When you focus on things you don't control, how 'in control' can you feel?

Let's say you really want a certain job. What do and don't you control?

Well, ultimately, you don't control whether or not you get the job. That is in your NO POWER ZONE. What IS in your POWER ZONE? Your energy, your effort, your attitude. So focus on what you control and then learn to accept the outcome. The interesting thing is that when you work on what you DO control, you have more influence over the outcome, so you feel more powerful, and you often put your best foot forward.

Control vs. Influence

When you start to complain about the government...STOP! What good does complaining do? The government is in your NO POWER ZONE. But you always CONTROL how—or whether—you think about the government. You choose whether you complain, let it go, or take action. And you could take action. You could use time, energy, and money to try to INFLUENCE the direction of the government. You could even work up to a point where you have a lot of INFLUENCE. But even then, all you will ever have is INFLUENCE. No matter who you are, you will never CONTROL the government.

The same is true for people. Although you don't control other people, they may choose to be INFLUENCED by you. Some people accord you a lot of INFLUENCE, while others will hardly notice you. The people who are closest to us often allow us to INFLUENCE them the most. But remember, you don't control their thoughts and actions. They choose how much INFLUENCE you have in their life.

Ingrid Bergman (1915–1982), an internationally acclaimed actress, once said of her terminal cancer: "I have accepted it and will make the most of what's left of my life while I can. Cancer victims who don't accept their fate, who don't learn to live with it, will only destroy what little time they have left." In saying this, she focused on what she did control—her thoughts, her attitude, and the way she lived the rest of her life—rather than focusing on what she didn't control: her terminal cancer and the length of her life. She honored her power by focusing on the part of life that was within her power, the part of life in her POWER ZONE. How might her final years have been different if she had given her power to the cancer and worried about how long she would live? Would focusing on her NO POWER ZONE have improved her life?

When we have a problem, it's important to recognize our role in it. We may not have created the problem, but now that it is OUR problem, it's up to us to find OUR solution. While the problem may be in our NO POWER ZONE, the solution is often in our POWER ZONE.

The company you worked for was bought, and everyone was laid off. You could focus on how unfair this is...how times have changed and this wouldn't have happened in the past...how disruptive this is to your life...and on and on. You could see the problem as being out there, with the company, with bad business practices, with the state of the economy and the world. But you don't control any of these, so when you focus on them, you feel powerless. Complaining about what has happened to you makes you see yourself as a victim.

How powerful and in control can you feel if you are focusing on things that are out of your control?

Instead, you could own the problem and focus on your own attitude and actions. You could accept that it doesn't matter whether it's right or wrong, it just 'is,' and now you have to decide what you will do about it. You could understand you are not responsible for the problem, but you are responsible for your solution. So this is your problem, own it, and work on the part of the problem you control. Work on yourself and your attitude...and work on your resume, look through job announcements, call family and friends who might be able to help. Take action. Now how in control do you feel?

> **Change is not merely necessary to life— IT IS LIFE.**
>
> *Alvin Toffler, American Writer and Futurist (1928–)*

When you blame your problems on something or someone else, then you look to them to change and/or you feel sorry for yourself. Neither of which improves your life. When you wait and complain, nothing changes.

When you own your problem, you focus on yourself and how you think and act. You work on your attitude and you take action. You make changes. You are actively involved in solving your problem. So things do change.

As someone once said, "The more time we spend blaming our circumstances on others, the more time we waste, [be]cause while we were blaming, we could've been doing." When you blame, you focus on your NO POWER ZONE. When you act, you operate in your POWER ZONE.

> When you own your problems, you retain your POWER. And when YOU change, your LIFE changes.

So, if you don't like the way a friend is acting, you could focus on them, wonder what is happening with them, complain about them, and be upset and think about how they should change. (NO POWER ZONE)

—Or—

You could focus on yourself and how you could handle this problem, working with your thoughts and attitude and adjusting the amount of time or power you give them in your life, in your story; you could take action by changing the way you interact with them. (POWER ZONE)

So you have a choice—you could complain about this friend and wait or hope he changes, or YOU could change. You could change how you think about him and the situation, how much time and power you give him in your mind, how you deal with him, and how much time you spend with him. As a result, he may change. But if not, then you choose again how and when you interact with him. Either way, your relationship will change. And it will change because you changed.

> Success is the ability to go from failure to failure without losing your enthusiasm.
>
> *Sir Winston Churchill, English Statesman and Author (1874–1965)*

When you want life to change, don't look outside; look inside. You make the change.

When you make a mistake, you could focus on the past, thinking about it and being angry at yourself for the error. But you can't change the past. It is in your NO POWER ZONE.

Instead, focus on the present. Focus on what you CAN do to correct the mistake, and/or focus on what you can learn from this experience. Work with your thoughts and attitude, and learn to accept and respect yourself as a fallible human being. Now you are operating in your POWER ZONE.

When you focus on your NO POWER ZONE, you feel powerless and weak, you see life as out of your control, and you see yourself as a victim.

When you focus on your POWER ZONE, you take control of your life. You recognize and claim your power, and as a result you feel strong and in control.

When you start to worry about...

...an airplane crashing...STOP! You have NO POWER (unless you're the pilot).

...someone talking about you...STOP! You have NO POWER.

...all the possible things that could be happening to someone who is late...STOP!

Don't waste your time and emotional energy on things you can't control.

Focus on what you CAN control. Focus on yourself, your thoughts, and your attitude. Determine if there are any actions you can take to improve the situation, and if there are, take them. But remember—you don't control the outcome.

Thinking of all the ways a friend should change = NO POWER ZONE.

Figuring out ways you can change your attitude and the way you deal with this person = POWER ZONE.

> **Problems are only opportunities in work clothes.**
>
> *Henry J. Kaiser, American Industrialist (1882–1967)*

To claim your power, focus on what you CAN CONTROL!

Focus on your POWER ZONE.

Generating Power–Making Healthy Choices

So focusing on what you control helps you recognize your power. (P+)

Creating positive stories adds power. (P+)

Taking action feels powerful. (P+)

Believing and living by the Six Sensible Rules adds power. (P+)

1. Things won't always go my way.
2. I'm not perfect, but I'm still okay. (I am a perfectly imperfect human being.)
3. Sometimes people do things I don't like.
4. Life isn't always fair; it's just life.
5. I recognize that I don't really know much at all.
6. I choose my life.

All this helps you create thoughts that are **Optimistic** (P+), **Rational** (P+), and **Accepting** (P+). Thoughts that are positive and powerful.

Your thoughts and actions can generate a sense of power in your life where you feel happy, confident, involved, comfortable, in control, and POWERFUL!

But your thoughts and actions can also leak power, leaving you feeling down, unsure, lost, out of control, and POWERLESS.

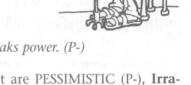

Trying to change or control something you don't control, leaks power. (P-)

Creating negative stories leaks power. (P-)

Waiting leaks power. (P-)

Fighting life leaks power. (P-)

Complaining and feeling sorry for yourself leaks power. (P-)

All this helps you create thoughts that are PESSIMISTIC (P-), **Irrational** (P-), and **Critical** (P). Thoughts that feel negative and powerless.

Power–	Power+
Pessimistic ◆ It will never work. ◆ I can't do it. ◆ That won't help.	**Optimistic** ◆ I'll figure it out. ◆ We'll get through this. ◆ Things will be better. ◆ We'll find a solution.
Irrational ◆ But they have to do what I want. ◆ It has to be fair. ◆ I shouldn't have frustrations. ◆ Life should be the way I want.	**Rational** ◆ I don't expect life to be fair and for things to always go the way I want. ◆ I can't do anything about them. But I can do something about me.
Critical ◆ I'm so stupid. ◆ People are so selfish. ◆ They shouldn't act like that.	**Accepting** ◆ Life isn't going to be perfect and neither am I. ◆ I will appreciate what I have in life.

You go through life generating power and leaking power. And how powerful you feel is based upon your own particular mix. Minute-by-minute, thought-by-thought, action-by-action you can either add to your sense of power or reduce your sense of power.

Your attitude and actions can either help you claim your power or reflect your sense of weakness.

So to be the most powerful YOU that you can be, not only do you want to…

GENERATE MORE POWER,

but you also want to REDUCE YOUR LEAKAGE.

Approach it from both directions.

Add a little power here. "I can do this. Just take one step at a time. One. One. One. …"

Patch a leak there. "I HAVE to be selected. I have to get this chance, otherwise…. Wait, wait, wait! Just because I WANT it to happen doesn't mean it has to happen. I can live without this. Heck, there will be other opportunities in my life. Two years, or even two months, and I could be totally over it. Let's get on with life. I'll do what I can to influence the outcome and then accept that what will be, will be."

Add a sense of power: "Sure I want her to like me, but I'm going to have fun either way."

Patch a leak there: "Rats, another stop light. Now I'm really late. Move people, MOVE! …Stop! Take a deep breath. I'm musting again. People must move! Why? Because that's what I want. I must not be late. Why? It might work best if I weren't late, but it's not the end of the world. These people shouldn't be so slow.

> When you blame others, you give up your power to change.
>
> *Dr. Robert Anthony,*
> *Personal Performance*
> *Trainer and Author*

Why not? Besides, it's not their fault I'm late. I could have left earlier. Plus, 100 years from now will this matter? 10? 1?"

Add: "So, what can I get from this? How can I turn this into an opportunity?"

And patch: "I NEVER do anything right. Wait. That's not true. How do I feel when I think that thought?"

Add optimistic, rational, and supportive thoughts. Add POWER.

Question and rethink the negative, irrational, and critical thoughts. Patch the leaks.

Add and patch. As you do, you will build a sense of power. You will develop a rational attitude that is optimistic and accepting and feels powerful.

Little Drips Can Turn into Big Leaks

We all leak power. Sometimes it's in drips and other times it's a steady stream. But even those steady streams began as a little drip, a little drip that grew. If we had patched this leak when it first began, it would have been easier. But now repair will take much more work, much more patching and generating of new power.

Recently a friend of mine started focusing on his negative thoughts. He repeated them, added to them, and allowed them to alter his view of everything. He dredged up old memories that validated these thoughts and ignored any that didn't. Within a short span of time he had dug himself into such a negative mood that it took him days to climb out of his funk. And it all started with him and his own thoughts.

Most of my friend's thoughts were about being unhappy because life wasn't going the way he wanted. (Isn't that what most of our complaints are about?) He then blamed his unhappiness on other people, thinking of the many things they did that he didn't like and the many ways in which they 'should' change.

But if your happiness (or unhappiness) is based on others, you have no control. What if instead he had taken control of his thoughts and happiness? What if when he first began to have negative thoughts he had stopped himself and said, "Wait a minute. What am I doing? Where is this leading me? Do I want to go there? What am I focusing on? Could I turn my focus elsewhere instead?"

What if he had asked himself the four questions from *The Work* by Byron Katie:

◆ Is this true?

◆ Can I absolutely know that this is true?

◆ How do I react when I believe this thought?

◆ Who would I be without this thought?

What if he had stopped exaggerating? What if when he thought, "She always...or they never..." he had instead thought, "This isn't true"?

What if when he made irrational musty statements, he had simply asked himself, "Why? Why must it go the way I want? Why must they like what I like? Why does he have to be the way I want him to be"?

It's not just one or two negative thoughts that drain our energy; it's many of them. So that gives us many opportunities to question them and choose again. Learn to stop your negative thoughts early, before they snowball on you.

> For a long time it had seemed to me that life was about to begin—real life. But there was always some obstacle in the way. Something to be got through first, some unfinished business, time still to be served, a debt to be paid. Then life would begin. At last it dawned on me that these obstacles were my life.
>
> *Fr. Alfred D'Souza*

Learn to take control of your life. Only when you accept responsibility for your thoughts, your actions, and your life do you truly become free.

Recently I watched two people have a parking lot war about who pulled in front of whom. They did not seem to know each other. But both of them stopped in the middle of their day and spent 15 minutes angrily yelling, and I'm sure they continued to fume long after they left. Do you think this is really what they had planned for their day? Do you think they really wanted to waste part of their day focused on someone they will most likely never see again, arguing about some issue that—in the grand scheme of things—is really of little importance? Did they claim power over their lives, or did they let other people and the situation hijack them?

This is what claiming your power is all about. Claiming power in your life. Taking your life in the direction you want to take it and not letting situations, events, and especially other people take it to a place you really don't want to go.

Yelling and arguing may look powerful from the outside. But in reality, that sort of behavior represents someone who has let their thoughts and emotions spin out of control or who is using their anger to manipulate (or both). They have not learned to claim their power. In fact they are giving their power away.

We often give our power away. A little bit here and a little bit there, and it all adds up. Our language is a good indication of this.

Watch Your Language

If you are upset with someone and you say, "He made me mad," what does that really mean? He MADE you? You didn't have a choice? He controls your feelings? You may think you don't mean that, but your words indicate that you do. Just like the people in the parking lot war, you chose to let another person's actions influence your mood. And a clear indication of that is the statement, "He made me mad." Once upon a time 'he' did something that you didn't like and you chose to think negative, critical thoughts that caused you to be mad. But where are those thoughts? And who controls them? You do, unless you give this power away.

People use so many phrases that indicate they have given away part of their power,

from saying they have to wait for something to happen to be happy ("I'll be happy when I get done with this.")

...to blaming others for their mood or even their life ("It's stressing me out," or "She ruined my life.")

...to simply feeling sorry for themselves because life didn't go the way they wanted. ("Why did this have to happen to me? Poor me.")

The message is, "I'm not in control. Other people or things cause my feelings. And what happens to me controls my life." Talk about giving away your power!

In fact, scientists looking for trends in victimology analyzed the front page of the October 1st editions of *The New York Times* over the last 60 years and found a steady erosion of the notion of personal choice and a steady increase in the notion of being a victim. When you see yourself as a victim, you stop focusing inside of you and what you can do; instead you focus outside of you and what has 'been done' to you. You stop being an active director in your life and become a spectator; a spectator complaining about the direction of your life. And as Dr. Martin Seligman, past president of the American Psychological Association, noted, "There is a strong relationship between passivity and depression."

So watch your language. It reflects your thoughts and your attitude. Learn not to give away your power. Watch for:

Waiting Statements

"I'll be happy when he leaves, when I have more money, when I get what I want."

"I can't wait until I get a better job."

"I can't be happy until I lose weight, or find someone who loves me."

"Life will be good when...."

When you wait for happiness, or love, or for success to come your way, you stop claiming power over your life. But who is in charge of your happiness? Who decides what you focus on, think about, or pay attention to? Who is choosing to wait for happiness? Take back control.

Blaming Statements

You can blame a momentary mood on something or someone:

"They made me mad."

You can blame a life pattern on something or someone:

"I keep picking losers. I've got bad luck."

You can even blame your whole life on something or someone:

"It's my parents' fault that I'm so messed up."

When you BLAME, you point away from you and towards something or someone else and give them responsibility for your feelings. "Goodbye POWER!" More blaming statements:

"He bothers me." (He controls my feelings.)

"She really gets on my nerves" (She controls my feelings too.)

"I would have done better if my teachers had encouraged me." (Their actions determined my life. It's none of my doing.)

"They hurt my feelings." (Who has the power here?)

"It's their fault that I...." (I'm not responsible for my choices.)

"I don't have time." (I don't even get to choose how I use my time.)

Instead of blaming, take action. Change something; change your thoughts, or change your actions. When you change, your life changes.

Self-Pity Statements

POOR , POOR PITIFUL ME !

"It's not fair."

"Why me?"

"Not again."

"Nobody loves me. Everybody hates me. Guess I'll go eat worms." (And then complain about them the whole time I'm eating them.)

— Poor Poor Pitiful Me, song by Warren Zevon, (1947–2003) American Musician & Songwriter

And does feeling sorry for yourself improve your life in any way? Are you taking action or just wallowing in your misery?

Weak or Indecisive Statements

"I'm not sure I want to." (Same thing.)

"I don't know if I can do that." (Do you really not know, or do you just not want to commit?)

No Control Statements

"I really don't want to." (Now, does that mean you won't, or that you still might do it, even though you 'really' don't want to?)

"I can't stop thinking about it." (You can't control your thoughts?)

"I couldn't help myself." (You can't control your actions either?)

Demanding Statements

"I have to have...a boyfriend..." (This controls your happiness?)

"I have to do this right."

What happens if you don't get what you demand? We often use these words or phrases without realizing that by using them, we are giving away our power.

Little by little, every time we do that with words and deeds, we drain our spirit. So learn to use words that convey a sense of power and control in your life. Because when it comes to your sense of power, every little drop counts. Watch Your Language

The Two Sides of Please or ASKING vs. PLEADING

When you say, "Please stop it," you are asking someone to change. Since people prefer being asked, rather than told, it's important to start your requests with the word PLEASE. But if you've made the same request several times, and your requests are being ignored, using the word

"please" becomes more of a plea, a plea for them to change their behavior, a plea that is being ignored. The other person is not respecting you or your wishes.

You could complain, feel sorry for yourself, and blame the other person. But why don't you go with your POWER instead. ACT!

STAND up for yourself

STATE your position

STAY CALM and respectful

REPEAT your statement

REMOVE yourself from the situation

Do The Little Things

Changing the direction of your life, changing the way you think and feel can seem overwhelming. But you don't have to do it all in one giant leap. As an old saying goes, "Rome wasn't built in a day."

Recently, a friend started walking a couple of times a week. I asked if he was trying to get in shape. He stated, "yes." But he wasn't going on a big exercise binge. He was just going to walk a little more and eat a little less. He was going to approach it from both directions.

Now, if you think about it, doing a little in both directions can add up to a major change.

So just do the little things. Catch a musty thought here. Change an exaggeration to a rational thought there. Notice when you use language that gives your power away, and rephrase your statements. Add a little power here and eliminate a leak there. Little by little, you will build yourself up to where you recognize and claim your power. And you become the most powerful you that you can be.

I can't change the direction of the wind,
but I can adjust my sails to always reach my destination.

Jimmy Dean, American Singer, Actor, and Businessman (1928–)

Success is not the key to happiness.
Happiness is the key to success.
If you love what you are doing, you will be successful.

Albert Schweitzer, German Physician, Philosopher, and Theologian (1875–1965)

Peace is a daily, a weekly, a monthly process,
gradually changing opinions, slowly eroding old barriers,
quietly building new structures.

John F. Kennedy, 35th President of the United States of America, (1917–1963)

The pessimist complains about the wind;
the optimist expects it to change;
the realist adjusts the sails.

William Arthur Ward, American Scholar and Author (1921–1994)

It is not easy to find happiness in ourselves,
and it is not possible to find it elsewhere.

Agnes Repplier, American Essayist (1855–1950)

The meaning of our existence is not invented by ourselves,
but rather detected.

*Viktor Emil Frankl, Austrian Neurologist, Psychiatrist,
and Holocaust Survivor (1905–1997)*

12

Sailing

What do you want from life? How do you want your life to be?

There could be thousands of answers to that question, and most of them would involve wanting to be happy, wanting to feel good about yourself and your life.

That's what most of us want.
We want the same thing!

We want to feel happy, proud, special, important, and confident.
We want to feel powerful.
(We'll just take them all, thank you.)

So how or where do you find this happiness?

Well, let's go sailing.

219

Sailing

Imagine you are sailing your life's ship towards happiness.

Your skills were developed over the years and are a result of your temperament mixed with your environment and experiences. You learned 'on the job.' So what did you learn? Did you pick up baggage? (More important, do you still carry it?) What type of stories do you tell about life? Did you develop a rational thinking style? Do you question negative thoughts? Do you work with your feelings? All these contribute to how you sail your ship.

So how do you travel? How do you get from place to place?

Well, you have sails. You can wait and catch favorable winds (opportunities) that blow your way. These winds will help you sail towards your goal.

But what if there are no winds? Or what if they are blowing in the wrong direction? You don't control the winds. You don't control the seas either. What if while you are waiting for the right wind, a huge storm (an obstacle) crashes in, tosses you around, and even knocks you off course? That won't help you reach your goal.

*But wait! You don't have to rely on the wind. **YOU can generate power!***

You generate power with your thoughts—thoughts that help you navigate your ship. Positive stories help you move forward. Thoughts that are optimistic, rational, and accepting help you move forward. Thoughts like these focus forward on what you can do and things you can control—things in your POWER ZONE. With this power you can go any direction you choose. You don't have to wait for the right wind to blow you in a certain direction. You can even go find favorable winds (besides, waiting is passive). With favorable winds and your own power, you can make real progress. Plus you can travel when there is no breeze. And NOW you can better handle those storms. Since you are focused on your sailing instead of the storm, the storm doesn't become an obstacle blocking your view. In fact, your attitude and actions help you avoid many storms, and others you just learn to power through to get beyond the turbulence. And with your own power, you WILL get through.

This ability to create optimistic, rational, and accepting thoughts is a powerful thing.

But what if you don't generate much power?

In fact, what if you create leaks?

What if your thoughts are negative, irrational, and critical? Now how far and fast can you travel? Can you make your ship move the direction you want, or do your thoughts hinder your progress? Can you even take advantage of favorable winds, or do your negative thoughts weigh you down? Do you have enough power to get through storms or are you stuck inside?

LIFE IS LIKE SAILING

When you generate optimistic, rational, and accepting thoughts, YOU feel powerful. You control the direction of your life. You can watch for opportunities and you can create new opportunities. And since you are focusing on yourself and working at maintaining a positive yet realistic attitude, your own thoughts aren't creating obstacles. When you do encounter storms, you can focus on your sailing and not let the storms dominate your life. You focus on what you control. You focus on things in your POWER ZONE. So you learn and do what you can, and you keep going. You don't control the environment; you never will, but you can control yourself and how and where you sail.

On the other hand, when you create pessimistic, irrational, and critical thoughts—thoughts that leak—you will have difficulty moving towards happiness no matter what. Any forward movement is counteracted by negative thoughts. And even when you catch an opportunity, your negative, unrealistic thoughts will slow you down, halt your progress, or even push you backwards. And sure, storms present difficulties, but your own pessimistic, irrational, and critical thinking is what turns difficulties into obstacles. The more you focus on these obstacles, the more you let them block your view. In fact, your thoughts can turn almost anything into an obstacle—an obstacle that dominates your trip.

When you create leaks, you use a lot of energy fighting life, and you seem to go nowhere. Some people become so discouraged that they give up trying to reach any goal and just float adrift. Some people even want to jump ship. Let's hope they seek help and take sailing lessons instead.

So how do you decide which way to sail?

Which Way Is Happiness?

Well, that depends upon whom you ask, or rather, whom you listen to.

Let me explain.

When you focus on your power, you focus on yourself, your thoughts, feelings, and actions. You pay attention to you, how you feel, what you want, what feels right. With optimistic, rational, and accepting thoughts you are OPTIMISTIC, RATIONAL about, and ACCEPTING of yourself. So to make your decisions, to decide which direction to sail for happiness, you consult YOURSELF. You provide an INNER COMPASS, your inner guide. You make choices that reflect your interests and abilities and that you think will work best for you. You are sailing in a manner that reflects your sense of power, and you are sailing in a direction that is best for you. You create happiness. And you do it by consulting you.

When you leak power, your time is spent in negative, musty thinking focused mainly on your NO POWER ZONE. So first, your own complaining, demanding, exaggerating, worrisome, angry, questioning, or unsure thoughts ARE DOMINATING YOUR TIME. (How can you even hear yourself think, let alone feel with all that racket?) And second, when you are more focused on your connection to the world outside, this is often where you turn for your answers. So where do you look for happiness? Well, maybe you can find it in that new outfit…or the new job…or a girlfriend…or money…or a fancy house? Happiness is out there; you just know it must be.

But will you really find happiness OUT THERE?

Happiness is an inside job.

Listening to Ourselves

We usually 'know' what is best for us, but if our mind is really busy, we don't hear the message. Later, when things don't go as planned, we may remember that we had 'a feeling' but chose to ignore it. We didn't want to hear it. The message came from our inner voice of wisdom. Our mind had other plans.

Maybe that's the problem.

Messages from our inner wisdom come through our feelings. They come through our awareness of our body. But what takes up most of our time? Our mind.

✦ ✦ WHAT IF WE MAKE A WRONG TURN?

Sometimes we worry that we will make a mistake or won't go the 'right' way.

First, worrying is a result of musty thinking: "I must be perfect. I must not mess up. I must make the right choice." Guess what? You are going to make mistakes. Life is full of mistakes, little ones and big ones. You're human.

And second, there is no 'right' way. Every direction you choose can help. Either it helps you move towards a personal goal or it offers a life lesson that can help you make decisions in the future. So sometimes you learn what to do, and sometimes you learn what not to do. And if you don't learn, you will continue to make choices that cause you to repeat the same type of mistake again and again and again, until you DO learn.

So what if life goes off course? What if there are storms all around or you get temporarily stuck in dry dock? Is there any chance of happiness?

Happiness isn't tied to the direction you sail. It's tied to the way you sail: how you think, how you handle your problems, how you handle your life. You could have everything in the world (well, maybe not everything) and still be unhappy and struggle with life. And you could have nothing, yet appreciate life and be happy. So which do you do more, fight life or appreciate it?

✦

Life Does Not Have to Be Perfect to Be Wonderful.

Annette Funicello, Singer, Actress, and 'Mouseketeer' (1942–)

Sure, some people were dealt opportunity cards and some were dealt storms. Sure, life isn't fair. But no matter what cards you are dealt, YOU choose how you play your hand and how you sail your life.

As Viktor Emil Frankl (1905–1997), an Austrian neurologist, psychiatrist, and Holocaust survivor, once said, "We who lived in concentration camps can remember the men who walked through the huts comforting others, giving away their last piece of bread. They may have been few in number, but they offer sufficient proof that everything can be taken from a man but one thing: the last of the human freedoms—to choose one's attitude in any given set of circumstances, to choose one's own way."

Be Gentle

Be gentle with yourself and others. We are all still learning how to sail.

We all developed some bad sailing habits growing up. And it can take a long time to let go of these old self-destructive habits and develop new healthier habits. We do it little by little, thought by thought, moment by moment.

Learn to be accepting; not just of life, but of yourself and others.

At times you will leak energy: you will think pessimistic, irrational, and critical thoughts; you will focus on your NO POWER ZONE; and you will sail in unhelpful directions. You are human. This just means you still have work to do, more thoughts to question. These are your lessons. So learn what you can from each of them.

At times other people will leak energy: they will think pessimistic, irrational, and critical thoughts; they will focus on their NO POWER ZONEs; and they will sail in unhelpful directions. Others are human, too. They still have work to do. They have their own life lessons.

Each of us is doing the best we can.

Don't you think if we knew how to sail better we would?

And realize, we may all be aiming for happiness, but just like love, sometimes people look for happiness in all the wrong places.

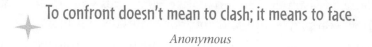

To confront doesn't mean to clash; it means to face.

Anonymous

The only thing we have to fear is fear itself.

Franklin Delano Roosevelt,
32nd President of the United States of America (1882–1945)

When we hate our enemies, we are giving them power over us:
power over our sleep, our appetites, our blood pressure, our health,
and our happiness. Our enemies would dance with joy if only
they knew how they were worrying us, lacerating us, and
getting even with us! Our hate is not hurting them at all,
but our hate is turning our own days and nights
into a hellish turmoil.

Dale Carnegie, Author and Speaker on Personality Development (1888–1955)

Courage is resistance to fear, mastery of fear–not absence of fear.

Mark Twain, pseudonym of Samuel Langhorne Clemens,
American Author, Humorist, and Social Observer (1835–1910)

When you hate, the only person who suffers is you.
Most of the people you hate don't know about it,
and the others don't care.

Medger Evers, American Civil Rights Leader (1925–1963)

Always forgive your enemies; nothing annoys them so much.

Oscar Wilde, Author (1854–1900)

13

Handling Power Seekers

The POWER SEEKERS

People like to feel powerful because, well, it feels powerful. And, sometimes people look outside themselves for ways to help them feel special, important, or powerful. They think if they get the latest gizmo, are the best at something, become part of a 'special' crowd, win contests, etc., those things will increase their sense of value.

But sometimes people **use** other people as a way to gain power and prove their supposed superiority. They put people down, push others around, or act like they are more important than others. They want to PROVE they are POWERFUL. These are POWER SEEKERS.

Here are some potentially hurtful ways people try to gain power:

◆ Talk about and make fun of others;
◆ Put someone down;
◆ Manipulate things so they always come out 'on top';
◆ Bully and push people around;
◆ Hurt others;
◆ Use anger to manipulate or hurt;
◆ Highlight others' flaws or mistakes;
◆ Gossip and start rumors;
◆ Boss people around;
◆ Trick, tease, or manipulate others;
◆ Scare and intimidate others;
◆ Force their way and opinion on others.

You occasionally may have done things like these to try to make yourself look good or make others look bad (which we in turn think makes us look good). But for some people this is their main source of feeling important. They thrive on the artificial sense of power they get by seeing themselves as superior or hurting or pushing others around.

So, what can you do if someone is doing this to you? What can you do if someone pushes you around, highlights your mistakes, tries to intimidate you, makes fun of you, or teases or hurts you in an attempt to gain control of (or feel superior to) you and/or others?

First, recognize that their behavior reflects them and their need for power. Try to Observe rather than Absorb their negative behavior. Keep in mind that their actions express their needs or wants. When people feel inwardly powerful they don't need to try to gain power OVER you or others. So, since their behavior tells about them, DON'T take it personally. It isn't about you. You don't play any part in their **need** for power. The only part you could play is if you look like an easy target. If you look weak, a power seeker will be attracted to you.

Second, and most important, focus on yourself, your power, your importance. Work on generating your power and eliminating leaks. When you feel powerful, it won't matter what the other person does, you won't let them affect your attitude or actions. You will Observe, not Absorb.

◆ Sure, what they did wasn't fair. But does complaining that it's not fair make it fair, or does it just make you miserable? Does it change them and the situation, or does it just change you and encourage feelings of sadness or anger?

◆ You didn't deserve to be treated like that. Heck, nobody does. But again, does this type of thinking make it better, or does it just make you feel more like a victim?

So who are you hurting when you feel like a victim? When you think like this do you feel strong or weak?

And if you say you feel strong because you get angry, where is this anger, and who is it hurting? Anger may feel strong but it's like a poison in your system. You can't be the best you as long as you carry it. Besides, it doesn't take brains to get angry. In fact, the angrier you get the more you shut down your Thinking Brain and operate on pure emotion. You may prove your physical strength, but you have given away power over your thoughts and emotions.

Think about it: when someone gets really angry—they may look POWERFUL. But are they really POWERFUL or are they using anger to try to look, feel, or prove they are? What do you think?

Think about how Martin Luther King, Mother Teresa, the Dalai Lama, Nelson Mandela, or Mahatma Gandhi would have handled things. Would they have used physical strength or inner strength to handle this situation? Would they have let this person dictate or dominate their emotions, or would they maintain control themselves?

If you leak energy with negative, fearful, critical, and pessimistic thoughts, your sense of power will be low. You won't be strong enough to ward off other people's attempts to gain power from you, and you will more likely focus on, and get caught up in, their negative energy.

So question and release your fears and demands so you can accept and respect yourself and life. When you do this, you exude confidence, you won't look like an easy target, and you won't let the other person's negativity drain your energy.

That may be all well and good, but what are some actual things you can do when people try to use you to prove their power?

LEARN NOT TO GET CAUGHT–DON'T BITE. SWIM FREE.

When someone sends a negative message your way, imagine that it is bait. They are fishing in an attempt to catch you, to get you to pay attention to them, or to have some power over your feelings or actions. If you bite, you are now on the end of their line. You have given them power over you.

It can be so easy to get caught up in their negativity and focus on them and their bait. But instead, why not just swim around their bait and continue on with your life? Don't Bite. Swim Free.

Here are some actual things you can say and do:

◆ Don't react. Basically ignore what they did or said. Don't get upset. Just walk away or say things like, "Whatever," or, "That's interesting." Then go back to what you were doing. Act like it's NO BIG DEAL. It only becomes a big deal if you make it one.

◆ Change the subject to talk about something else. If they say, "Did you hear me? I called you a jerk," simply say, "Yeah, I heard you." Then change the subject and talk about something else. You can even try to initiate a conversation with them by asking them about something ("I heard you got a new car. What did you get?"), complimenting them ("I really liked the way you..."), or just speaking nicely to them.

(continues on next page)

(continued from previous page)

◆ Agree with them (even if you don't). Say, "Yep, you're right. Uh huh, uh huh, yep, yep. Thanks for telling me." You can even agree that sometimes, maybe, they could be right. "Yep, sometimes I am." "Maybe you're right."

◆ Use humor. Make a joke out of what they said. Be sure not to make fun of them, though. If they think you are trying to show them up, this might only increase their need for power. So laugh at yourself or the situation. If they say, "You idiot," you say, "Well that's an improvement. Last week I thought I was a moron. You wouldn't believe what I did."

◆ Act like their negative statement is just an observation or a comment and thank them for sharing with you. "Why, thank you. I didn't know that." Make sure you don't sound sarcastic, but instead, like you really do appreciate the feedback.

◆ Ask questions. Be curious about their behavior or words, "Why would you say that?" Or, "I'm confused." Or, "Why does it matter to you?" Or, no matter what they say you could just keep asking, "Why?" Act genuinely curious, not sarcastic.

◆ Stand up for yourself without getting upset and/or attacking back. Just calmly stand your ground. Tell them what you want and don't want. Start your statements with 'I.' Say, "I don't want you to do that." Or, "I don't want to."

You could also add these words before you make your statement:

"It may sound crazy, but ..." "I would like to let you, but ... " "You might be right, but ..." "That could be true, but ..." "I'd love to, but...." You could also use an 'I' statement pattern: "I feel ____ when you ____, because _____."

Remember to:

1. Stand up tall;
2. State your position. Make it short and to-the-point;
3. Stay Calm and Respectful (of yourself and others);
4. Repeat, Repeat, Repeat your position if necessary; and
5. Remove yourself from the situation.

If you do any or all of these things, will they stop? Maybe...maybe not. Remember, you don't have power over them. They may keep harassing you because others are paying attention. Or they think they just have to bother you more to get a reaction. But if you Observe rather than Absorb, if you stay firm and calm and don't react, then you are not allowing them to determine your mood and your behavior. You haven't given away your power. You will look and be strong. You will stand up for yourself, which may include making changes to reduce your contact with people like this. Remember, what someone else says or does matters to you only if you decide it matters to you. You have that power.

Special Situations:

I was only kidding. Can't you take a joke?

You may encounter a person who pushes you around or teases you, and when you object, they act like YOU have offended THEM. Like they were innocent and you are the one with a problem. They will say things like, "Well, ssooooorrrryyy." Or, "What's wrong with you? Can't you take a joke? I was only kidding." Don't get caught in their game. Their game is to act without considering your feelings and then pretend they are innocent. If they were truly innocent, they would apologize. So stand your ground. Tell them how you feel and what you do or don't want. "I'm angry and want you to leave me alone." Repeat it if you need to. And if they try to convince you that there is something wrong with you, don't believe them. Feelings are neither right nor wrong, they just are. And how you wish to be treated is your choice, not theirs. So, don't:

◆ Get defensive, "I do too have a sense of humor."

◆ Make excuses, "I'm just in a bad mood."

◆ Attack them, "Well, if you would be more considerate...."

Just say, "That's how I feel and that's what I want."

It's your life. It's your choice.

Rumors

At times we talk about others. We may simply make a comment or point out a fact. But we also may hear or dig up dirt on someone and then spread it around. Whenever we speak negatively about someone, we are judging them. Judging others gives us a false sense of superiority. We see ourselves as above the person we are judging. Even if there is some truth to what is being said, do we really have a right to judge others? We have not lived their life from zero to now. We have no idea of the struggles they may have had, either internal or external. Besides, do we want them judging us? Remember to treat others the way you want to be treated.

So what do you do if people start talking about you? Maybe they point out what they see as flaws, criticize your actions, make derogatory comments, make assumptions, or start or continue rumors. What can you do?

For one, see the comment or rumor as a wave. If you add energy to the wave, it gets bigger, goes further, and lasts longer. So don't add any energy to the rumor, no matter how bad or big it is. If you don't add energy, it will die out sooner.

Stay calm. State the facts if you want to, but don't argue with someone about it or attack people who you think are spreading the rumor. This just makes the wave bigger. Often, the more you try to

argue and defend yourself, the more people talk...and you rarely change their minds. You get caught in a trap. You say, "It's not true." Then they say, "Yes it is." You say, "No it isn't." They say, "Yes it is." "No it isn't." "Yes it is." And on, and on. You have put yourself in the powerless position of trying to change someone else's mind. Don't waste your time or energy. They will believe what they want no matter what you say.

So, keep your head high and move on with your life. Your actions will speak louder than your words. If you made a mistake, well, join the rest of us. We all have regrets. Take the opportunity to learn from your mistakes and then let them go. Pick yourself up and move on.

If you want to question or confront the other person, make it simple and quick, and then drop it. You can say, "Well, do you believe it?" If they say "No," that may end it. But if they say "Yes," then say, "Well, you can believe what you want." And leave it at that. You might have to repeat it several times. Remember, don't get caught up in defending yourself. If you say, "Believe what you want," and then add, "But it's not true," then you are caught in the defensive argument trap: "Yes it is." "No it isn't." You will never convince them, so don't even try. Just leave it at, "Well, BELIEVE WHAT YOU WANT."

When People Abuse the Power We Give Them

When we envy, look up to, or want people to like us, we give them power, and this power can be corruptive. They can begin to believe that behavioral rules and courtesies don't apply to them. They learn that they can be mean and others will still follow along, look up to them, or even that the person they were mean to still wants to be their friend. They may even learn that they can break rules and their actions are ignored or forgiven. All this because others see them as somehow special, desirable, or important.

This happens in school, at the office, in a social group, and in society. The 'in' crowd—the cool, the pretty, the popular, the rich, and the athlete—are just some of the people to whom we often give this much power.

This happens in groups, but it can also happen on an individual basis. When you WANT someone to like you, you give them power over you. They can be rude and you are more willing to accept or forgive their behavior. They can boss you around and you do what they say. You may put up with many things just to be accepted or 'loved' by them. Or you will do anything to 'make' them happy or to avoid their anger or rejection. You discount your own wants, wishes, and feelings, and instead defer to them.

If you are in a situation where a group follows someone who exhibits disrespectful behavior, you can't change the group. You don't have power over others. But you do have power over yourself. You can decide not to follow them or participate in their negative behavior. You can stand up and voice your concerns. Or you could just slip away and connect with another group. If you stand up and voice your displeasure, others may agree with you, or the group may turn against you. And realize that others in the group may feel as you do but might not have the courage to stand up and say anything, so they continue to follow along.

In situations like this, standing up for what you think is right can be very difficult. Remember, when you express your concerns, don't attack, defend, or argue, just express your feelings and your preferences. You may not be able to change the situation, but you do have power over your own actions.

On an individual level you have a lot more power because you choose what type of relationship you are going to have with that one person. You can take back the power you gave them and stand up for yourself, demanding to be treated with respect. Here again, this works best if you don't attack, defend, or argue, but instead simply express your feelings and your desires and then stand your ground. And remember, you do not control the other person's reaction. They may start treating you with respect. Or they could try to pressure you (talk, beg, bribe, or try to punish or scare you) or pretend they were joking to try to get you to drop your demands. Or they could decide to stop associating with you. And if they don't treat you with respect, you can choose to stop associating with them too.

YO-YO FRIENDS

So when you really want someone to like you or you really want to be included, you give people power over you. Some people will still be respectful, but others will take advantage of this power. In the beginning they may do something slightly rude or offensive, and yet they see you still come back, wanting to be with them. They learn that they don't need to check themselves, consider your feelings, and modify their behavior. You may complain, but if you keep coming back, then your actions indicate you will allow and accept this behavior—you will put up with it. So now the pattern is set. They can be nice some of the time and rude at others. They may want you around, then want you to leave. Act like you are a good friend, and then get mad at you, and even act as though it was your fault. So it's back and forth, back and forth in the way they treat you. They pull you in, then push you out. You never know which way it will be. In and out, and in and out—like a yo-yo.

This is a yo-yo friend, and guess what? You are the yo-yo. Now, you could spend all day discussing the reasons they act as they do...but why waste your time? What is happening here? They pull you in and push you out as they want. Who has the power? They do. Who is in control? They are.

You may complain and want them to consider your feelings and be more respectful. But when they pull on the string, who comes back to them? You do! And who gave them this much power? You did! So why should they cut the string? They are getting what they want when they want it. So if you don't want this type of friend, if you don't want this type of relationship, don't go back. CUT THE STRING. They can't pull you in and continue to yo-yo you if there is no string attached. Move on and find a true friend.

When Things Get Physical

Usually physical intimidation, abuse, or attacks don't just suddenly appear. Normally, there are warning signs well before someone gets physical in an effort to gain power, get what they want, or hurt you. Maybe the other person makes threatening comments or their tone gets increasingly rude or hostile. Maybe they pressure you to do as they wish or start trying to control you, telling you how you should act and who you should be with. They may even start nudging, grabbing, or pushing at you as they get more and more demanding. Any or all of these actions could precede actual physical violence.

The best time to stop this aggressive behavior is when you first get an uneasy sense, a gut feeling, that something isn't right. Your intuition—your own personal early warning system—is telling you to be cautious; this person is not safe. If you recognize, listen to, and then honor your intuition, you will take actions to reduce or eliminate the problem before it escalates. You will either let the other person know this behavior is unacceptable and set boundaries, or you will limit or even eliminate contact with them. The longer you let people like this behave as they choose, the harder it is to resolve this problem.

Too often people don't honor their intuition. They downplay, rationalize, or ignore this gut feeling. They say things like:

◆ "He didn't mean to hurt me. That's just the way he is."
◆ "If I say something, she may stop being my friend."
◆ "It was an accident."
◆ "This (the other person's jealous, controlling behavior) just shows how much they care for me."
◆ "He only did it because...."
◆ "I kind of deserved it."
◆ "She really is sorry."
◆ "It won't happen again."
◆ "But he really loves me."
◆ "What would I do without them?"

People say these types of things and allow the aggressive or violent behavior to continue.

People also put off dealing with this problem. They wait for the 'right' time, for the next incident, or for things to get worse before doing something, all the while allowing this disrespectful and dangerous behavior to continue.

They worry that they are overreacting or that they will offend the other person or lose them as a friend. But if you find someone's behavior worrisome, you are not overreacting; it's how you feel. Your feelings reflect your sense of comfort. Your feelings deserve respect.

If you're worried about offending the other person, stop and ask yourself, "Are they worried about offending me? So who am I thinking of? Them. And who are they thinking of? Themselves. So who is thinking about me?"

And if you lose them as a friend—well, were they the type of friend you really want?

Don't limit yourself. Many people limit themselves to what they think they can do. You can go as far as your mind lets you. What you believe, you can achieve.

Mary Kay Ash, U.S. Business-woman—founder of Mary Kay Cosmetics, Inc. (1918–2001)

If you do nothing because you are afraid they might hurt you even more, then this is definitely a time to REMOVE yourself from the situation and seek outside help. Contact the authorities. If you do NOTHING it WILL get worse. So do something NOW.

But how did it get to this point?

You ignored all the early warning signs sent out by your intuition.

Learn to recognize and honor your intuition so this doesn't happen. Put a stop to aggressive behavior before it gets out of hand.

✦ ✦ **RETALIATION**

What does it look like?

One day, while you are driving towards your future, Person 'A' cuts too close in front of you. Now she could have done it on purpose, or she could have been careless, or stressed over an emergency, or rude and inconsiderate, or simply didn't see you. Which story do you want to tell? It's your call. You may never know the truth (and even if you think you know, you don't know the whole story). Let's say you decide she is being rude and inconsiderate and you start thinking musty thoughts. "How dare she do that to me. Who does she think she is? She should be more considerate." So now you get angry, very angry, and decide to get back at her. So you speed up and cut her off. Now she pulls up next to you and starts yelling. So you speed up and try to cut in front of her again. But this time you don't quite make it and you crash. Your day is shot, and the life you planned is interrupted for weeks. Plus, you've got extra expenses and a bureaucratic hassle. And you are still angry at the other person. All this adds up to make your life better, right?

> The more anger towards the past you carry in your heart, the less capable you are of loving in the present.
>
> *Barbara De Angelis, Author and Motivational Speaker*

Or it could have gone this way.

One day, while you are driving towards your future, Person 'A' cuts too close in front of you and cuts you off. You reject any musty thoughts and decide not to make up a story. She cut you off. You've done that occasionally, either in driving or in life. And you've done it for a variety of reasons, some of them mentioned above. So you just back away from Person 'A' and keep driving. Later, you hardly remember it happened.

(continues on next page)

(continued from previous page)

Days later you have been many places, and you are miles down the road towards your future. Now how did these choices add up?

> **Be kind, for everyone you meet is fighting their own battle.**
>
> *Adapted from Plato, Greek Philosopher (427 B.C.–347 B.C.)*

The first example is what retaliation looks like. Instead of continuing to drive the direction you want and having a chance to get somewhere, you become sidetracked. You spend time and energy focusing on the other person, planning and thinking about how to get back at her. And even if you don't crash, as in the story above, you wasted a lot of time thinking negative and vengeful things. Whatever time you give this person in your mind is time taken from your life, your future. Negative thoughts create negative energy. Planning revenge is "like taking poison and waiting for the other person to die." It hurts you first, long before it ever has a chance to hurt the other person. You have stopped going in a positive direction—focusing on your life, your goals, and your talents—and instead you spend time thinking negative, vengeful 'musty' thoughts about what happened that take you nowhere. You have given the other person a leading role in YOUR story.

Remember, the most important thing about forgiving is that it helps you. You release your grip on negative things from the past (and remember, even a second ago is the past) and are now free to go your own direction, create your own life.

How Do You Let People Treat You?

You don't control other people. But you do control you. And if you put up with bad behavior or physical or emotional abuse towards you, WHY?

If someone treats you poorly and you don't stand up for yourself, what did they learn?

So if someone does treat you poorly, speak up or do something to try to reduce the chance of it happening again. And if it happens again, say or do something else, or stop associating with this person.

People put up with bad behavior for many reasons:

◆ They really want a person or a group to like them or at least include them;

◆ They are caught off-guard, or are confused, or afraid;

◆ They think they caused it or deserve it;

◆ They have allowed it before, so now how do they stand up and say, "No more";

◆ They don't think they deserve any better or that this is the best they can get;

◆ They think they can save or change the other person.

It doesn't matter if you have allowed that behavior in the past, you have the right and the responsibility to yourself to stand up at any time and say, "NO MORE. I will not put up with this behavior any longer."

> They say the chains of habit are too light to be felt until they are too heavy to be broken. The chains you put around yourself now have enormous consequences as you go through life.
>
> *Warren Buffett, Investor, Businessman, and Philanthropist (1930–)*

If you continue to put up with being treated poorly, what are you saying about yourself? If you truly respected and valued yourself, would you allow this behavior? Who decides what you deserve and what you don't deserve?

If you accept poor treatment from others, then you are telling them loud and clear with your actions that you don't truly believe you deserve any better.

So make your actions strong. DO NOT STAY in a situation where someone treats you poorly. Stand up for yourself and leave. You are too good for that.

Remember, no one has a right to hurt you physically. This behavior is inexcusable and unlawful. Contact the authorities to protect yourself,

> The difference between the impossible and the possible lies in a person's determination.
>
> *Tommy Lasorda, U.S. Baseball Pitcher and Manager (1927–)*

to protect others, and hopefully to even get help for the person who handles life with violence.

You choose your friends. So, if you choose to interact with someone who treats you poorly, why do you continue to see them? Choose another friend.

You don't choose your family. But you do choose how you think, how you act, how you treat yourself, and how much contact you have with them. No matter what someone says or does, you are important and special. And if someone treats you otherwise, that reflects him or her, not you.

When Bullies have POWER— Dealing with People in Authority

Power corrupts, and absolute power corrupts absolutely.

Lord Acton, British historian (1834–1902)

Or maybe it's more like this:

Power does not corrupt. Fear corrupts...perhaps the fear of a loss of power.

John Steinbeck, Author (1902–1968)

As we all know, sometimes people in authority abuse their power. Whether they become abusive because they have so much power or because they are afraid of losing their power (or both) doesn't really matter. What does matter is that somehow they start seeing themselves as above others.

So how do people in authority end up being bullies? Well, some of them were Power Seekers to begin with and then just moved into positions of power. And some people didn't intend to become bullies (and may not even see themselves as bullies), but then they moved into a position of power, and it became easy to start pushing people around or putting others down.

The important thing to remember is that just because someone is in a position of authority doesn't mean that they are any better or deserve more respect than you or anyone else.

What are some positions of authority where people can slip into displaying abusive and bullying behavior?

Bosses, supervisors, teachers, coaches, police officers, church authorities, older siblings, parents...basically anyone who is in a leadership position or who sees themselves as having more power or being in charge in a situation.

Now, just because someone in charge tells you what to do, that doesn't make them a bully. Sometimes people who are in charge are going to tell you what to do. That's their role.

Plus, sometimes coaches, teachers, parents, and others try to motivate through intimidation, negative pressure, or fear. Their goal may be admirable—to try to get you to do your best—but their method may be disrespectful. Still, some people find this behavior pushes them to improve while others view it as degrading.

Each person decides for himself or herself what feels comfortable and what doesn't. Generally, though, there is a difference between being responsible and trying to motivate, and being a bully. If there is an attempt to humiliate, degrade, take advantage of, intimidate, abuse, or push others around, then the person's behavior has crossed the line from being in charge or motivating to being disrespectful and possibly even abusive.

So how do you respond when a person in power acts like a bully? There is no single right answer, but here are some suggestions.

◆ Focus on your attitude and behavior. Always treat others with respect no matter how they treat you. Remember, your actions reflect you. Your respectful attitude will carry you through many difficult situations.

◆ If the behavior is not that offensive or you will have minimal contact with this person, you might choose to ignore the offense and just remove yourself from the situation.

◆ If the person is in a position to cause you more trouble, be extremely nice and then get out of the situation as soon as possible. Questioning or challenging will only escalate the confrontation. And in most cases you are the one who will suffer the most from this.

◆ If you have ongoing contact with the person, you may choose to talk to him or her about how you feel and what you want. And as mentioned earlier, you do not need to defend yourself, make excuses for how you feel, or attack the other person. Just state how you feel and what you want or don't want.

◆ If you believe that talking to the person would be fruitless and the behavior is offensive enough, you may choose to speak to his or her supervisor. If you do this, make sure you have exact information on what transpired (time, dates, exactly who said what to whom, etc.), and report the facts.

◆ Remove yourself from the situation as soon you can. Move to a different job, change departments, drop the class, leave the team, etc. You may have to give up something you truly like to maintain your dignity.

◆ If a person's behavior is threatening or physically abusive, remove yourself immediately and contact a higher authority.

Remember, your value is determined by you and not by the way others treat you. So whatever you choose to do, do it with dignity and respect. Keep your head high. Things may work out well, or things may not turn out the way you want (such as what might happen if you confront a popular coach). But always know that you were true to yourself and treated yourself with dignity and respect.

✦ ✦ PARENTS AS BULLIES

This can be a very difficult situation. Some parents are naturally bossy, because that's what they learned. Some parents are naturally respectful, because that's what they learned. Most parents are a little of both.

Physically abusive behavior, even by parents, needs to be addressed and stopped, which may include contacting authorities. Because children grow up, become physically and emotionally stronger, and move away, physical abuse rarely continues into adulthood.

Emotionally abusive behavior can be equally detrimental, but since it is not as obvious (i.e., there are no physical marks), it can be harder to confront. Emotionally abusive behavior includes things like consistently criticizing and berating, name-calling, being overly controlling and bossy, or giving a person frequent silent treatment. Emotional abuse can continue throughout a lifetime. Some parents are adept at using the manipulative tools talked about in Chapter Two to get their children (even their adult children) to do what they want. They may beg, bribe, or try to make you feel bad, guilty, sorry, or scared, or pressure you to get you to do what they want. Remember, their behavior has nothing to do with you. It has to do with what they learned and how they think about life and themselves. Like a Me-Me, they are often thinking only about themselves.

Success doesn't come to you...you go to it.

Marva Collins, Honored Educator (1936–)

When I hear somebody sigh, "Life is hard,"
I am always tempted to ask, "Compared to what?"

Sidney J. Harris, Author (1917–1986)

The pessimist sees difficulty in every opportunity.
The optimist sees the opportunity in every difficulty.

Winston Churchill, English Statesman and Author (1874–1965)

I haven't failed. I've found 10,000 ways that won't work.

Benjamin Franklin, American Printer,
Author, Diplomat, Philosopher, and Scientist (1706–1790)

The art of life isn't controlling what happens,
which is impossible; it's using what happens.

Gloria Steinem, American Writer and Political Activist (1934–)

Every choice moves us closer to or farther away from something.
Where are your choices taking your life? What do your behaviors
demonstrate that you are saying yes or no to in life?

Eric Allenbaugh, Psychologist, Leadership Consultant and Author

14

Your Travel Guide

We've traveled bumpy roads and climbed mountains. We've been to the bottom of the sea and we've sailed atop the waves. We've talked thought cycles and consulting our INNER COMPASS. We've talked about snowballs, onions, soup, baggage, playing cards, parking lot wars, stolen cars, roller-coaster rides, eating cookies at airports, and Buddhist farmers and their horses. All of this designed to help us learn how to make better life choices and learn how to create happiness.

> **You were born an original. Don't die a copy.**
>
> *John Mason, Author and Speaker (1955–)*

You are the one who creates happiness in your life. You don't have to rely on others or wait for your life to change in order to be happy. When you change your attitude and the way you approach a problem, you can change your life. You can even change your luck.

AS LUCK WOULD HAVE IT

Professor Richard Wiseman of the University of Hertfordshire in England conducted a study that showed you can learn to be lucky. The following approaches improved a person's luck:

1. Maximize Chance Opportunities–Open Your Mind.

Lucky people are skilled at creating, noticing, and acting upon chance opportunities. They do this in various ways, which include building and maintaining a strong network, adopting a relaxed attitude to life, and being open to new experiences.

2. Listen to Your Lucky Hunches.

Lucky people make effective decisions by listening to their intuition and gut feelings. They also take steps to actively boost their intuitive abilities—for example, by meditating and clearing their mind of other thoughts.

3. Expect Good Fortune.

Lucky people are certain that the future will be bright. Over time, that expectation becomes a self-fulfilling prophecy because it helps lucky people persist in the face of failure and positively shapes their interactions with other people.

4. Turn Bad Luck into Good–Look Towards the Upside.

Lucky people employ various psychological techniques to cope with, and even thrive upon, the ill fortune that comes their way. For example, they spontaneously imagine how things could have been worse, they don't dwell on ill fortune, and they take control of the situation.

From The Luck Factor: Changing Your Luck, Changing Your Life—The Four Essential Principles *by Dr. Richard Wiseman*

What's more, people who participated in a program to help them change their thinking improved their luck.

Most of the time luck doesn't just miraculously appear; you have to keep trying for luck to 'happen.' What looks like luck is often just extended effort with a positive attitude. If you keep your chin up, keep taking risks, and put in focused effort, then you will create luck simply because the more things and times you try, the greater the opportunity for luck to present itself. If you try only once, you have only one chance at hitting that 'lucky opportunity.' But if you try five times you have five chances. Thus, it makes sense that people who keep their chins up, are optimistic, and keep trying are going to be luckier. And those who get down, are pessimistic, and give up easily are not.

> **Do or do not; there is no try.**
>
> *Yoda, Star Wars Jedi Master*

Which description fits you? Do you keep trying or give up? Or even more important, which do you want to be?

Now notice I said 'focused effort.' Effort alone is not the answer.

Once a fly was in a room that had several windows. One of the windows had a screen with a hole in it. The fly flew furiously around the room, bumping into everything. It expended much energy but didn't escape from the room. But all along there was this one hole it could easily have flown through to gain its freedom.

Energy alone is not the answer. You need to look around, assess the situation, relax, consult your intuition, and then take action. Make sure your effort is focused and directed so you don't just run around knocking into one obstacle after another.

POST VIEW

The Basics

All day long you make one choice after another, and your choices add up. Most big choices don't just suddenly appear. They are the result of many little choices along the way. So, if you want your life to head in a different direction, start taking little steps in that new direction. Some choices are easy but others are very difficult. And when you feel stressed it's hard to think clearly. In fact, the more stressed you feel, the more your Thinking Brain shuts down. And you need this Thinking Brain to help solve complex social problems. But your Thinking Brain also creates a lot of problems with its ability to worry, guess, wonder, and basically think. You will make mistakes—sometimes big mistakes. Everybody does. What's most important is what you choose

to do after you make them. GETTING MAD AT YOURSELF DOESN'T HELP. Getting mad at yourself for something you have already done doesn't change the past; it only affects how you feel and act in the present. And if you stay upset, that will affect the future.

Pressure from People

Sometimes people try to pressure you into doing what they want. They talk and talk, bend the truth, bribe, beg, act real nice, or involve others to increases the pressure. They may try to make you feel bad, guilty, sorry for them, or too scared to oppose them. They may even try to force you to do what they want. And if their trick works and they get what they want, they will keep pressuring you. But remember, they are thinking only of themselves. They are ME-MEs. So who are you thinking about? Are you more worried about them and what they think, or are you thinking about yourself and what is best for you. Remember, their Outside Pressure doesn't work without your Inside Pressure. And you control the Inside Pressure. So when people pressure you, learn to SHUT THE DOOR.

Remember to:

- Stand up for yourself,
- State your position,
- Stay Calm and Respectful,
- Repeat your position, and if you need to,
- Remove yourself from the situation.

And don't forget your rights. You have the right to:

1. Feel the way you feel;
2. Say "No";
3. Change your mind;
4. Think differently from others;
5. Say, "I need time to think," and to think as long as you need (without pressure from them);
6. Say, "I don't know";
7. Offer no reasons or excuses to justify your decision.

Thoughts, Options and Choicycles

No matter what happens, you choose how you act. You have lots of choices and it all starts with you and the way you think and feel. You have developed habits in the way you think. If you have a habit of thinking optimistic, rational, and accepting thoughts, then this is how you most likely handle problems. If you have a habit of thinking pessimistic,

(continues on next page)

(continued from previous page)

irrational, and critical thoughts then this is how you most likely handle problems. And although feelings came first, you now use your thoughts to describe, analyze, and even create your feelings. How you think and feel affects how you see things, which then affects how you act. And how you act affects what happens to you. It's a Choicycle.

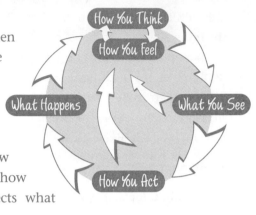

Adjusting Your Personal Radio Station
Adjusting the Messages You Play in Your Head.

Don't believe everything you think. Remember, you just made up those thoughts in your head. So if your thoughts cause you pain, create new ones. And learn to catch your negative thoughts early, before they have a chance to snowball on you.

Notice the stories you tell about your life. Your story could offer a negative, pessimistic view or a positive, optimistic view of your life. It's your choice. But remember, how you feel, what you notice, and how you act are all affected by the stories you create. So basically, you create your life by the way you think.

If your thoughts cause you pain, question them. Use the questions developed by Byron Katie:

Ask Yourself:
1. Is this true?
2. Can I absolutely know that this is true?
3. How do I react when I believe this thought?
4. Who would I be without this thought?

Learn to accept life as it is. Learn to play the hand you were dealt. Because if you fight what IS, if you fight reality, you lose. You lose out on happiness because reality isn't going to change. Besides, why would you fight a battle that you could never win? Talk about feeling powerless!

And remember to focus on what you want in life, because what you focus on grows.

Get REAL-Be SENSIBLE

We create most of our unhappiness by exaggerating, having unrealistic expectations, and demanding that life be the way we want. So watch out for 'musty' thoughts: "I MUST...." "They MUSTN'T...." "It SHOULD...." "Life SHOULDN'T...." "I HAVE TO...." "They NEED TO...." 'Musty' thoughts turn our wishes and preferences into DEMANDS.

Be realistic about yourself, others, and life. There will be ups and downs. Everyone has problems. People won't always do what you want. You will encounter It's NEN people. Things won't always go the way you want. You are never going to be perfect—so just accept yourself as you are. Life isn't going to be fair—it's just life.

Remember the Six Sensible Rules:

1. Things won't always go my way.
2. I'm not perfect, but I'm still okay. (I am a perfectly imperfect human being.)
3. Sometimes people do things I don't like.
4. Life isn't always fair; it's just life.
5. I recognize that I don't really know much at all.
6. I choose my life.

(continues on next page)

(continued from previous page)

And if you find yourself being irrational and fighting life, ask yourself, "Why? Is this helping me? Is what I'm doing making my life better, easier, or happier?"

Dropping Unpleasant Feelings

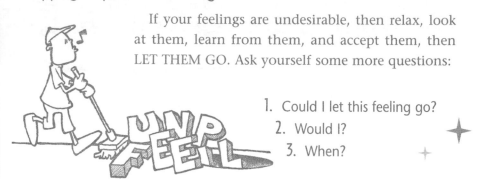

If your feelings are undesirable, then relax, look at them, learn from them, and accept them, then LET THEM GO. Ask yourself some more questions:

1. Could I let this feeling go?
2. Would I?
3. When?

Repeat this set of questions until you feel a shift in your feelings. (from *The Sedona Method®*)

Work back and forth with your thoughts and feelings. Question your negative thoughts. Then focus on your accompanying feelings and try to release some of the intensity. Then question your thoughts again. Then focus on your feelings. Back and forth.

Learn to forgive. Holding on to negative thoughts and memories hurts you the most. Forgiveness is not about helping the other person; it's about helping you live a happier life. It's about releasing the hold that these negative thoughts have on your life so you can move forward.

Feeling down and sorry for yourself does nothing to improve your life, so work on your thoughts and focus on what you CAN do. And remember, your emotions can take you on a wild roller coaster ride. So if your emotions are out of control, or if you are stuck at the bottom, get help!

Here are some numbers you can call:

1-800-273-8255 (1-800-273-TALK)
1-800-784-2433 (1-800-SUICIDE)

Making Your Best Decision

Making decisions that honor and work best for you involves many factors. Keep healthy. Reduce the pressure you feel from others and yourself. Drop unpleasant thoughts and feelings.

And it also helps if you try to adopt a positive, loving, and appreciative attitude towards life. So sing, smile, tell positive life stories, and

learn to be grateful. Remember, focusing on your heart and FEELING grateful, appreciative, and loving is probably the most important thing you can do to improve your outlook on life. Because what you focus on grows. So try to grow more appreciation and love.

Also, learn to relax, breathe properly, and begin to notice the messages from your body. Meditate to help you feel centered, balanced, and open to your knowledge from within.

Honor Your Intuition

We all have intuition; we just need to learn to access and use it. Your intuition can help you with decisions such as which job to take, but it can also save your life. Most intuitive messages are subtle. Learn to recognize them and honor them. Don't let your mind take over and win the argument against them. Remember, your best information about you comes from within you.

(continues on next page)

(continued from previous page)

A Look in the Mirror

Each person's thoughts, feelings, and actions reflect that person. So your side of a double-sided mirror reflects you, and the other side of the mirror reflects others. If someone treats you poorly, says negative, mean, cruel things to you or about you, it doesn't say a thing about you. It tells about them. Your thoughts, feelings, and actions reflect YOU. So realize that no matter how someone treats you, you control your side of the mirror. You have power over the way you view yourself. You have power over your life. You can choose how you think, feel, and act. So don't focus on the other side of the mirror, just work on your side. Happiness and confidence are inside jobs. Remember to Observe, not Absorb. Observe other people's behavior; just watch, don't judge, and try not to Absorb their negative mood or messages. Look at them through a lens; don't be a sponge.

Traveling Tips

Your personal style is based upon your own particular soup mix. The soup base is your temperament, and then experiences are added as you go through life. We all pick up baggage along the road of life. Some of it is passed down from generation to generation. If you are in a family that passes on negative baggage, learn to let it go. First let it go for you, so your life will be happier, and then let it go so you stop passing it on to others. How you think about a problem determines whether you see it as a mountain or a molehill. How you think about a problem determines how much time it takes up in your life. No matter what type of adversity you face, there have been others who faced similar problems and survived and thrived. But there have been others who crashed and burned. Which group will you be in? Learn to survive regardless of your situation. Start your climb today and keep your eyes on the road.

More Power to You

To be the most powerful you that you can be, focus on what you control. Stay in your POWER ZONE. Focus on yourself, your thoughts, feelings, and actions. The more time you spend thinking about people and things in your NO POWER ZONE, the more you give away your power. Besides, how powerful can you feel when you focus on things you have no power over?

Make healthy choices. Choose thoughts that generate power and avoid those that leak. Create thoughts that are optimistic, rational, and accepting, and question and release thoughts that are pessimistic, irrational, and critical. And remember, all big leaks started as one little drip; question your leaky thoughts early so they don't snowball on you.

Watch your language; it is a clear indication of how much you give away your power. No person or event can MAKE you mad. Being mad is a choice you make based upon your thoughts. Rephrase exaggerated, demanding, and musty statements and take back your power. And remember, changes don't happen overnight. It takes years to change some habits. So don't worry about making big changes, just Do The Little Things. Catch a musty thought here. Change an exaggeration to a rational thought there. Notice when you use language that gives away your power and rephrase your statements. Add a little power here and eliminate a leak there. Little by little you build yourself up to where you recognize and claim your power. And you become the most powerful you that you can be.

(continues on next page)

(continued from previous page)

Sailing

Life is like sailing. Optimistic, rational, accepting thoughts create power that helps you move towards your goal. And pessimistic, irrational, critical thoughts leak power and slow your progress. Whether you reach your goal or not is up to you.

To help you decide which direction to head and what's best for you, learn to consult your Inner Compass. You are the expert on you. And remember, happiness isn't found in your destination. Happiness is created by the way you travel.

Handling Power Seekers

Sometime in your life you will encounter people who use their positions to try to prove their power. They use their power to put you down or push you around. You can't change these people—you can't change anyone but yourself—so don't focus on them. Work on your side of the mirror. The more you recognize your power, the less you let others affect you. Learn not to 'take the bait.' Remember, you teach others how to treat you, so stand up for yourself and don't give away your power. Always reflect respect.

Minute by minute, thought by thought, you choose your life.

So what kind of life will you choose?

- ◆ Will your life be full of peace or turmoil?
- ◆ Will you be optimistic and focus on what actions you can take, or will you be pessimistic and focus on what has been done to you?
- ◆ Will you respect yourself and others, or will you be critical and judgmental?
- ◆ Will you live with love and appreciation or turn towards anger, resentment, jealousy, and hate?
- ◆ Will you take responsibility for your life, or will you blame others for difficulties and stumbles?
- ◆ Will your thoughts and actions lead towards a sense of purpose and feelings of success? Or will you see yourself as struggling and unsure of your direction?

It's your life. It's your choice.

You are in the driver's seat. You have many choices to make because there are many directions in which you can travel. Any path you choose will have ups, downs, bumps, and detours. Your thoughts, attitudes, and approaches determine the smoothness of the road and how (or if) you get past obstacles. You choose whom you travel with and whom you avoid. And all of these choices determine the direction your life takes. You can stay in the driver's seat, or you can choose to let others control the wheel. It's all your choice.

I hope you choose to have a nice trip.

From when you are very young, to when you are very old, life is one choice after another, after another, after another, millions and billions and zillions of choices.

The choices you make add up to make YOU!
So Choose the Life you want.
Choose YOUR Life.

The End
(Or Is It the Beginning?)

My attitude towards life will determine
life's attitude towards me.

Anonymous

The future is not some place we are going to, but one we are creating.
The paths are not to be found, but made, and the activity of making
them, changes both the maker and the destination.

John H. Schaar, Teacher, Writer, and Scholar

Don't say you don't have enough time. You have exactly the same
number of hours per day that were given to Helen Keller, Louis Pasteur,
Michelangelo, Mother Teresa, Leonardo da Vinci,
Thomas Jefferson, and Albert Einstein.

H. Jackson Brown Jr., Author (1940–)

If you think you're too small to have an impact, try going
to bed with a mosquito in the room.

Anita Roddick, British Businesswoman, founder of The Body Shop (1942–)

All the adversity I've had in my life, all my troubles and obstacles,
have strengthened me.... You may not realize it when it happens,
but a kick in the teeth may be the best thing in the world for you.

Walt Disney, Cartoonist, Movie Producer,
and Theme Park Designer (1901–1966)

Never let the fear of striking out get in your way.

Babe Ruth (George Herman Ruth, Jr.)
Major League Baseball Star (1895–1948)

Index of
Quotes, Poems and Lyrics

263

Index

responsibility, 161, 259
retaliation, 239–240
rights, personal, 35, 251
rules to live by, 101
rumors, 233–234

S

sailing analogy, 220–222
Sedona Method / Sedona Training
    Associates, 109–110, 138, 254
self-confidence / self-esteem, 171.
    See also confidence
self-pity, 120
Seligman, Dr. Martin, 213
sensible, being, 73
shutting the door, 30–34
silence, inner, 140
smiling, 129, 167, 255
Steele, David Ramsay, 77
stopping your thoughts, 61
story, life, 55–58, 68, 69, 115, 116,
    159, 205, 207, 221
    changing, 121
    others', 117–118
    positive and negative, 97, 111
strength, 89
    personal / inner, 111, 229
stress, 8, 9, 13, 133, 250
    hormones, 59
    reactions to, 11–12
    reducing, 136
style, 256. *See also* temperament
success, 80–82, 218, 246, 259
support network, 248
Survival Brain. *See* Primitive
    Survival Brain
surviving / survivors, 183, 185,
    186–187, 257
sympathy, 166

T

teasing, 232

teen pressures, 28
temperament, 174–176, 180, 220
thinking / thoughts, 158, 251–252,
    257. *See also* negative thoughts
    and actions, 50, 205
    catastrophic, 119
    changing, 53
    as a cycle, 40–41, 45, 47
    dark, muddy, 48. *See also* negative
    and emotions, 103
    and feeling, 40–42, 44, 46, 113
    irrational, 74, 77, 95, 114, 127,
        208, 210, 221, 222, 257, 258
    musty, 77, 78–100, 223, 224, 239,
        240, 253, 257
    out-of-control, 59–62
    problems with, 54–55
    ways of, 39, 42–44, 50
Thinking Brain. *See* Rational
    Thinking Brain
Thomas, Alexander, 174
time
    pressure, 7
    wise use of, 167
tricks, 18–21, 30–31, 34–35. *See also*
    manipulation
truth, 75, 149, 151

V

victims, 185, 204, 213
violence. *See* aggressive behavior

W

waiting statements, 214
wisdom, 136, 224
Wiseman, Richard, 248
Wizard of Oz, 152
words. *See* language
worrying, 60–61, 85, 104, 111,
    119–120, 163, 177, 198, 223,
    224
writing thoughts, 150

End Note

I wrote this book on how to handle life, so I must have it all together, right? No. But I'm healthier today than I was last year, and as I remember and apply these skills, I will be even healthier next year. And remembering these ideas and skills seems to be the most important part. Often when I am in the middle of life, I forget about some of the things I have learned. I fall back into old unhealthy patterns. I may let my emotions take over and feel upset or sorry for myself. I may fight life and focus on things over which I have no control: things in my NO POWER ZONE. I even catch myself using phrases that suggest I don't control my emotions, thoughts, or actions. I'm still learning. I may work on some of these skills my whole life. But as I keep learning and remembering, I will get stronger. I will get better at accepting life as it is, consulting my inner core, and sailing my life in a good direction for me. I will claim more and more of my power. That's all I can hope for or expect. And that's life.

A Native American grandfather was talking to his grandson
about how he felt. He said, I feel as if I have two wolves fighting in
my heart. One wolf is the vengeful, angry, violent one.
The other wolf is the loving, compassionate one. The grandson
asked him, 'Which wolf will win the fight in your heart?'
The grandfather answered, 'The one I feed.'

Anonymous

What thoughts and feelings do you feed?

Place your order for:

Choose Your Life

A Travel Guide for Living

Paperback   978-0-9668530-7-0 $18.00

Make checks payable to: GR Publishing
Add 20% for shipping & handling
and 8.5% CA Tax (if necessary).
Quantity discounts available upon request.

MAIL your order to:
GR Publishing
PO Box 371
Felton, CA 95018

FAX your order to:
831-335-5333

E-MAIL your order to:
info@GRPBooks.com

ONLINE orders may be placed at:
www.GRPBooks.com

Children's Picture Books by Karen Gedig Burnett

••

Simon's Hook: A Story About Teases and Put-Downs (ages 5–12)

        Hardback 978-0-9668530-0-1 $14.95
        Paperback 978-0-9668530-1-8 $8.95

Katie's Rose: A Tale of Two Late Bloomers (ages 5–10)

        Hardback 978-0-9668530-2-5 $14.50
        Paperback 978-0-9668530-3-2 $8.50

The Magical Marvelous Megan G. Beamer:
A Day In the Life of a Dreamer (ages 5–10)

        Hardback 978-0-9668530-5-6 $14.95
        Paperback 978-0-9668530-6-3 $8.95

If the World Were Blind:
A Book About Judgment and Prejudice (ages 8–108)

        Hardback 978-0-9668530-4-9 $17.00